SHOULD I SHOULDN'T I
(start my own business)?

*To Margaret
Good luck!
Yanky*

YANKY FACHLER

Author of
Fire in the Belly – an exploration of the entrepreneurial spirit
Chutzpah – unlocking the maverick mindset for success

Published by TheExcellenceForum
www.theexcellenceforum.com

© 2007 Yanky Fachler

ISBN 978-0-9556704-0-4

All rights reserved.
No part of this publication may be reproduced or transmitted in any form or by any means, including photocopying and recording, without written permission of the publisher. Such written permission must also be obtained before any part of this publication is stored in a retrieval system of any nature. Requests for permission should be directed to
yanky@bookbuzz.biz

Printed in Ireland by ColourBooks

Dedicated to:

… all those who inspired me to choose the entrepreneurial path

… all those who are inspired by this book to choose the entrepreneurial path

… all those who felt I should have dedicated my previous books to them, especially Amy

… James, for believing in this book

… Mona, my constant inspiration

… my sons Ashi and Amiti

… my grandsons Uri and Nissan

Also by Yanky Fachler:

Fire in the Belly – an exploration of the entrepreneurial spirit (Oak Tree Press)

My Family Doesn't Understand Me – coping strategies for entrepreneurs (Oak Tree Press)

Chutzpah – unlocking the maverick mindset for success (Oak Tree Press)

The Vow – a biography of Eva and Eli Fachler (Trafford)

6 Officers, 2 Lions and 750 Mules (PublishAmerica)

CONTENTS

Introduction	1
Why do we all start out working for someone else?	7
QUESTION 1: Dare I leave the security of the employment world?	27
QUESTION 2: Do I trust the reason that has triggered my decision to go out on my own?	34
QUESTION 3: Can I cope with the reaction of my family?	60
QUESTION 4: Do I understand the difference in mindset between the world of employment and the world of self-employment?	73
QUESTION 5: Am I prepared for the downside of self-employment?	84
QUESTION 6: Am I the right age to start my own business?	94
QUESTION 7: Do I know in what field I want to make my mark?	99
QUESTION 8: Should I work from home?	107
QUESTION 9: What entrepreneurial qualities do I need?	113
QUESTION 10: Do I have the passion, the fire in the belly and the chutzpah?	131
Should I, Shouldn't I?	140

INTRODUCTION

At some point in their career, many salaried employees fantasise about starting their own business. If you had to guess at the percentage of the total salaried population that did this, what would you choose?

- ☐ 0% - 25%
- ☐ 25% - 50%
- ☐ 50% - 75%
- ☐ 75% - 100%

If you chose the last box, you're close to the mark. Most surveys across the industrialised world indicate that 80%-90% of all salaried employees share this fantasy.

That means that a lot more people than we realise are grappling with the "Should I, Shouldn't I start my own business?" dilemma. Almost everyone fantasises about saying goodbye to the world of employment and becoming self-employed. It is likely that one of the reasons you opened this book is because you too have entertained such fantasies.

But if so many people dream of going out on their own, where are they all? Why does only a small proportion of the working population put their money where their mouth is and actually implement their entrepreneurial fantasies? Most salaried employees may think about going out on their own, and may talk about going out on their own, but they never do.

Why not?

It could be a question of risk aversion. It could be a question of waiting for the right sort of entrepreneurial opportunity to present itself.

> *The saddest summary of a life contains three descriptions: could have, might have, and should have.*
> Louis E. Boone

But for some people, the fantasy doesn't get lost along the way. Even if you're not yet ready to commit yourself to becoming an entrepreneur, you are at least prepared to explore beyond the fantasy. Maybe something has happened to stimulate your entrepreneurial juices. Maybe something has happened that makes you more willing to consider the option of giving up your salaried job.

If indeed you are thinking (or thinking about thinking) of starting your own business, you're part of a definite contemporary trend. Economists, the media and business experts all agree that the sign of a healthy economy is when more and more people start their own businesses. Governments know that they need to encourage entrepreneurship if they are truly committed to boosting economic well-being.

One sign of the popularity of entrepreneurship is the growing demand for entrepreneurial training. In the US alone, no fewer than 1,500 colleges currently offer entrepreneurship courses designed to teach entrepreneurial techniques, to analyse business situations, and to stimulate and encourage the entrepreneurial drive.

If you have ever asked yourself what entrepreneurial skills you will have to learn, here's a useful exercise. Simply jot down your answers to these questions:

- What critical **management** skills do I need to start my own business?
- What critical **business** skills do I need to start my own business?
- What critical **time management** skills do I need to start my own business?
- What critical **people** skills do I need to start my own business?
- What critical **marketing** skills do I need to start my own business?
- What critical **access to funding** skills do I need to start my own business?
- What critical **tax-related** skills do I need to start my own business?
- What critical skill do I need to profitably **develop, market and deliver** a new product or service?

When you have completed your answers – *PUT THIS LIST ASIDE UNTIL YOU FINISH READING THIS BOOK!*

That's right. You won't need the list for now - because this book is **not about skills**. There will be plenty of time later to explore any entrepreneurship skills deficit.

I have nothing against entrepreneurial skills. Nor do I waste much energy worrying about whether entrepreneurship can be taught. I once got into trouble when I wrote an article ("Entrepreneurial training – red herring") in the *Journal of the Institute of Business Advisors*. I was accused by some readers of undermining all entrepreneurial education.

I think they missed my point. Starting your own business is much more than just the application of business skills to a new idea or concept. In my experience, most people – you included - are fully capable of mastering entrepreneurial skills.

But skills are just part of the entrepreneurial picture. In order to start your own business, you first need to make a mental switch from the world of employment to the world of self-employment.

Before you get into the "how" and "what" of starting a new business, you need to know whether you are fit to navigate the emotional transition from employee to entrepreneur.

> *No matter how successful you were in corporate America, you know nothing about becoming an entrepreneur.*
> Sigmund Goodwin

And that is what this book is about - your ability to adopt the entrepreneurial mindset.

When you finish this book, you may decide that you're not yet ready to make the jump. I still remember the young man who approched me at the end of one of my *Do I have what it takes?* seminars: "You have convinced me never to start my own business," he said. "It's far too much work." "Good," I replied, "I've done you a favour. I've probably saved you a heap of money that would have been swallowed up by your unsuccessful venture."

As much as I like to encourage people who want to take the entrepreneurial route, I acknowledge that not everyone has what it takes to become an entrepreneur.
But if you have a gut feeling that the entrepreneurial journey is worth exploring, this book will help you determine your own emotional fitness.

One of the triggers that prompted me to write this book was an email from a *Fire in the Belly* seminar participant:

> *Here's some food for thought. Last year, I completed my MBA at a prestigious university. I find it both ironic and absurd that the issues that you tackle, about what it takes or what it means to be an entrepreneur, were never even touched upon during my studies. When you think about it, this kind of discussion should be a basic part of any MBA. After all, you are dealing with people some of whom - myself included - see themselves as future entrepreneurs. What planet are these business schools on?"*

Richard Parkes Cordock completed his MBA in Monaco, and while he felt that the course adequately covered core business skills, he felt that there was too much emphasis on the employee mindset and too little on the entrepreneurial mindset. Believing that it takes a conscious effort to make the switch to the entrepreneurial mindset, Cordock created his Millionaire MBA home-study course.

Over the years, entrepreneurship support agencies in several countries have adopted and adapted the questions I pose in this book. These questions have also proved useful for training organisations and lending institutions that need an initial screening mechanism to help them determine whether people are emotionally ready for the nuts-and-bolts of entrepreneurial skills training.

Ultimately, whether you're a student, a thirty-something or a retiree, the real question is not whether entrepreneurship is right for you.

The real question is whether you are right for entrepreneurship.

> *Entrepreneurship finds many,*
> *but only the brave find entrepreneurship.*
> Suzanne Mulvehill

Why do we all start out working for someone else?

Have you noticed that we all start our working career as employees working for someone else? Look around. Everyone you know is now, or was in the past, employed. It's very rare to meet anyone who skipped the employee stage, and started their own business without ever having been employed by someone else.

This will change. I can safely predict that in the future, we will see more people who will question the need to experience employment before they embark on self-employment.

But for now, just about every self-employed person starts out as an employee.

Have you ever asked yourself why?

I believe that our school experiences provide a clue. Cast your mind back to your first day of school, an event that is eternally etched in your memory. You may have looked forward enthusiastically to that day, and retain many happy memories. You may have contemplated that day with trepidation, and retain traumatic memories.

But whether your memories of that day are positive or negative, have you ever asked yourself why you went to school in the first place? Why does everyone go to school?

When I pose this question in my seminars and workshops, I generally receive the following answers:

- **We go to school to learn**
- **We go to school to have fun**
- **We go to school to get an education**
- **We go to school to learn social skills**
- **We go to school to learn values**
- **We go to school to learn communication skills**
- **We go to school to make us mentally alert**
- **We go to school to expand our minds**
- **We go to school to gain knowledge**
- **We go to school because the law says so**
- **We go to school to learn sports**
- **We go to school because our parents want us to**
- **We go to school because we enjoy it**
- **We go to school to get qualifications**
- **We go to school to learn how to be grown up**
- **We go to school to prepare ourselves for life**

While all these responses make sense, I think there is a more fundamental reason for going to school, university, or other 3rd level educational establishments.

I believe that society makes a silent but effective pact with schools. Society tells the schools:

"We will build schools, we will pay teachers' salaries, we will pay you to take our kids off our hands from the ages of 5 or 6 to 17 or 18. During that period, you can educate them, teach them sports, teach them manners, or anything else on the list above. But whatever you do, you must guarantee one thing: that when these kids emerge from school, they are employable. They must be ready to be slotted into the job market. We have jobs to be filled. Your job is to produce employees who will take their rightful place in the world of employment."

From the day you start school, there is a well-orchestrated chorus of people encouraging you to believe that school is your passport to finding gainful employment.

- **Parents**
- **Teachers**
- **Faith leaders**
- **The media**
- **Business leaders**
- **Business organisations**
- **The government**

They all impress on you the importance of gaining qualifications that will help you get a job.

And when they say get a job, they always mean: get a paid job. When they talk about gainful employment, they mean working for someone else, finding a salaried position that provides security, stability, regular salary, career prospects, pension, and other social benefits.

Most people are quite happy to join the workforce and become productive and dedicated employees, filling job openings in manufacturing, retailing, service industries, academia, public service or other work sectors.

Receiving your first job offer is proof that your parents and your teachers were right. After all, didn't they always assure you that if you went to school and got your qualifications, you would find paid employment?

Your first day as an employee is a big event. All your years in the educational system have prepared you for this. You turned up at the office, shop, plant or other place of employment, proudly stepped over the threshold, and took your first step on the career ladder.

Exercise

- **Find a good sturdy stepladder**
- **Imagine that this ladder represents your first place of work**
- **Walk up to the ladder.**
- **Step on to the bottom rung.**
- **You have now entered the ladder world, the world of paid employment.**

FIRST DAY BLUES

- *A young man became a trainee in a big corporation. On his very first day at work, he dialled the canteen and shouted into the phone: "Get me a coffee, and make it quick!" The voice at the other* end responded, "Idiot, you've dialled the wrong extension. Have you any idea who you're talking to?" "No, who?" asked the trainee. "I'm the CEO of the company!" yelled the voice. The trainee yelled back: "And do you know who YOU are talking to?" "No," replied the angry CEO. "Good!" said the trainee as he slammed down the phone.

- Annette's first job was in a supermarket. She reported for her first day at work, and the manager greeted her with a warm handshake and a smile. He gave her a broom and said, "Your first job will be to sweep out the store" "But I'm a college graduate," Annette replied indignantly. "Oh, I'm sorry. I hadn't realised that," said the manager. "Here, give me the broom - I'll show you how."

- It is George's first day as a bank teller. A crusty old man comes to his window, and says "I want to open a damn checking account." George is taken aback by the old man's tone, and replies, "I beg your pardon, sir; I must have misunderstood you." "I said I want to open a damn checking account right now!" replies the old man. A distressed George calls over the bank manager, who asks the old man, "What seems to be the problem, sir?" "There's no damn problem," the man says, "I just won $10 million in the damn lottery, and I want to open a damn checking account in this damn bank!" "I see," says the manager, "and is this damn idiot giving you a hard time?"

Whether your first job is with a big or small employer, you now share several attributes with all other employees:

- **You are told what to do**
- **You are working for someone else.**
- **You receive a regular wage**
- **You are managed within a logical corporate hierarchy**
- **You look forward to steady employment and to the prospect of steady promotion if you perform adequately**
- **You share a set of expectations with your employer and your work colleagues about the nature of the employment deal**
- **Your job is at the mercy of others**

For your first few days on the bottom rung of the employment world, you're happy enough just being in a job. And once you become more familiar with your surroundings and with the office politics, you naturally start setting your sights on moving up the ladder.

You start thinking about opportunities for promotion. After all, how many people do you know who have zero ambition, and who want to remain on the bottom rung for the rest of their employment career?

The desire for promotion is normal for anyone who starts work in an organisation, big or small. Most people want to climb higher and higher on the promotion ladder. Promotion is a powerful form of validation.

Exercise

- **Stand on the bottom rung of the ladder**
- **Step up to the next rung**
- **You have now been promoted**

The process of acclimatising to the world of employment is normal - if you are happy to become an employee.

But what happens if you do not dream of working for someone else?

How does society in general, and the school system in particular, deal with people who dream of working for themselves? How do schools encourage entrepreneurial pursuits?

Unless you attended a really unusual school, the answer is: they don't. Encouragement of entrepreneurship is rarely part of any school curriculum. Most schools are not into entrepreneurship.

> *We are no longer judged by how smart we are, nor by how much training we've had. We are judged by how well we handle ourselves and each other in the workplace.*
> Daniel Goleman

Schools don't see their role as encouraging people to opt out of the workforce. Schools are not very good at answering the needs of those people who prefer to work for themselves.

Maybe it's no coincidence that so many successful individuals dropped out of school. Conventional educational and training institutions fail to hold much interest for people who think differently.

A well-known example is Richard Branson, founder of the Virgin brand, who describes school as "a place where grown-ups were just trying to keep us busy."

Here is a list of other famous people who dropped out of school:

- Soichiro Honda - founder of the Honda Motor Company
- Ray Kroc - founder of McDonald's
- John D. Rockefeller Sr - history's first recorded billionaire
- Vidal Sassoon - founder of the Vidal Sassoon brand
- Henry Ford - founder of the Ford Motor Company
- Mark Twain - American humorist
- Charles Dickens - English novelist and public speaker
- Thomas Edison – inventor of the incandescent light bulb and 1,093 patented inventions
- Noel Coward – singer, songwriter, entertainer
- Isaac Merrit Singer - sewing machine inventor
- Charlie Chaplin – actor, director
- Whoopie Goldberg - actor
- David Puttnam - Oscar-winning British film producer (Chariots of Fire, Midnight Express)
- Richard Desmond – newspaper publisher
- Charles E Culepeper – Coca Cola pioneer

Even American presidential candidates have managed to reach elevated positions without the benefit of a full school career. They include US president Andrew Jackson, New York Governor and presidential candidate Alfred E. Smith, and congressman and presidential candidate Horace Greeley.

A recent study compared the life ambitions of 4 year-olds and 18 year-olds. See if you can guess correctly their responses to the question: *Do you believe you can become anything you want?*

WHAT % OF 4-YEAR-OLDS BELIEVES THEY CAN BECOME ANYTHING THEY WANT TO BE?	WHAT % OF 18-YEAR-OLDS BELIEVES THEY CAN BECOME ANYTHING THEY WANT TO BE?
❏ 0 - 25% ❏ 25% - 50% ❏ 50% - 75% ❏ 75% - 100%	❏ 0 - 25% ❏ 25% - 50% ❏ 50% - 75% ❏ 75% - 100%

Would it surprise you to know that 96% of 4-year-olds believe they can become anything they want to be, while just 4% still believe this by the time they are 18?

These findings make perfect sense. Small children are often happiest when they are busily engaged in building, painting, playing games, inventing and creating. It is normal for pre-schoolers to demonstrate creative problem-solving abilities, a taste for risk-taking, and high internal motivation to succeed.

No wonder such a high proportion of children believe that the world is so full of possibilities.

Another study wanted to discover the extent to which youngsters are driven by their imagination. The study found that:

- **100% of 5 year-olds are driven by their imagination.**
- **10% of 7 year-olds are driven by their imagination**
- **2% of 20 year-olds are driven by their imagination**

In other words, between the age of 5 and 7, imagination as a driver falls dramtically from 100% to 10%.

The explanation for both these findings is that fundamental changes take place once children start school. As children enter the educational system, their creative, entrepreneurial spark is systematically ironed out of them. This is neither malicious nor deliberate, but it is the consequence of the almost exclusive focus on academic performance.

As a result, in the space of 14 years, we manage to disillusion nearly all our kids and convince them that they can't be anything they want. In the space of 14 years, we manage to knock the creative stuffing out of them. Once children reach adulthood, they are surrounded by people who are only interested in their credentials and qualifications, not in their aspirations and dreams.

The school system is not geared to give high priority to helping young people realise their full potential. The most important skill that many of us learn at school is how to pass exams.

I believe that if we are to support and facilitate entrepreneurial aspirations and endeavors among children, we need to make them more aware of the entrepreneurial option.

- We should encourage inquisitiveness by answering their questions by posing another question.
- We should encourage children to be more confident in solving problems alone.
- We should encourage children to make decisions about money from an early age.
- We should teach children the value of money.
- We should encourage children to understand the connections between work, salaries and taxes.
- We should listen actively to their opinions and suggestions.
- We should encourage children to understand that they can control their destiny and that they can affect the direction of their lives.

People are beginning to focus at last on the heart of the matter - let's teach entrepreneurship at school. School is where you prepare for the world of work, so why not learn how to work for yourself?
Peter Jones, serial entrepreneur, star of TV's Dragons' Den

It is ironic that during a child's formative first few years, parents watch and rejoice as the child develops its own personality, character, likes, dislikes and style of handling things.

But at the very point when kids reach autonomy, parents seem to take fright. At the very point when kids start acting freely, spontaneously, adventurously and with greater autonomy, many parents pull back the reins.
Studies show that 85 % of what kids hear from their parents is either what they mustn't do or how bad they are for doing it. Most of what kids hear is:

- "Don't do this!"
- "Don't do that."
- "Behave yourself!"
- "Do as you are told!"
- "Because I said so, that's why!"
- "Wait till your father hears about this!"

Things are not much better at school, where kids learn quickly that they need permission before they can go ahead and do things. From their first day in the educational system, they are taught to say: "Please Miss, may I go the bathroom?"

Children start learning that one of the most important objective measures of their own worth and value is someone else's opinion. They learn that their own needs must be subservient to the demands of authority. They learn that their value is measured by what it says on the school report card.

Having so recently formed their own individual assessment about the world around them, children now have to get used to a world that is governed by rules, regulations, conforming. They start losing the very qualities that defined their autonomy. They lose their spirit of adventure, their spontaneity and their freedom.

I can't help feeling that many schools are like battery farms. The chicken inmates are bunched up together in close quarters. The chickens lay eggs and are fattened up for the food chain. How different these chickens are from the Henny the Hen of our picture books. She clucked her way around the farmyard, pulling at a worm here, and drinking from a puddle there. She sniffed something the cows left on the ground here, and engaged in animated conversation with a goose there.

When people want an alternative to battery farmed chickens - they buy free range chickens. Why can't we have a free-range alternative for kids too?

Imagine how different things would be if the schools started producing more free-range kids. Imagine what sort of free-range adults they would grow up into. Imagine what would happen if kids received constant positive self-empowering feedback:

- "You are free and powerful!"
- "You will grow up and do great things!"
- "I have great confidence in you!"
- "Try and work it out for yourself."
- "I believe in you."
- "Go for it!"

Edward de Bono, the father of lateral thinking, has long championed the view that we should always respond positively. When someone says 2+2=5, we should say, "Great effort. Well done. Now let's see if there is an alternative answer."

While many people who progress from the educational system to the employment world enjoy their work, enjoy the people, and enjoy the career prospects, some people are not so lucky. They don't like their job. They want to change their job. There are many different reasons for wanting to change jobs:

- They don't get on with the boss or their colleagues
- They find the work boring
- They are not treated with respect by the boss
- They don't see advancement opportunities
- They think they'll be happier working for someone else
- They believe they'll earn more working for someone else
- They are lured away by the prospect of a better salary, better social benefits, greater responsibility and a bigger car
- They feel that they are not being given the opportunity to use their skills and abilities.
- They feel like a change
- They are head-hunted, poached or enticed by another ladder
- They are downsized or fired
- Their employer ceases trading

In a vibrant economy, it is relatively easy to decide to find another job, a better job. There is nothing strange or unusual about hopping off one ladder and hopping on to another. Everyone is doing it. There are very few people who have only ever worked for one employer.

Around the world, employee attrition rates have never been higher. People are staying for less time in their jobs. Surveys have showed that one third of the global workforce plan on leaving their jobs within two years.

Of course, if you are the recipient of comments like these actual comments taken from Federal Employee Performance Evaluations, then maybe you really should think about leaving your current employer:

- *This employee is really not so much of a has-been, but more of a definite won't be.*
- *He would be out of his depth in a parking lot puddle.*
- *This young lady has delusions of adequacy.*
- *He sets low personal standards and then consistently fails to achieve them.*
- *This employee should go far, and the sooner he starts, the better.*
- *He would argue with a signpost.*
- *Gates are down, the lights are flashing, but the train isn't coming.*
- *If you give him a penny for his thoughts, you'd get change.*
- *Takes him 2 hours to watch 60 minutes.*

Ladder hopping is a form of corrective action. There is no reason why you should remain stuck on a ladder that you don't like. Look for another ladder that will employ you. And another, and another, until you get it right. Most people eventually find their equilibrium, and settle on a ladder than suits them.

Exercise

- **Stand on the second rung of the ladder**
- **Step off the ladder completely**
- **Move the ladder to another position**
- **Step on to the second rung of the ladder**
- **You have now moved job**

Here is a tongue-in-cheek explanation for employee dissatisfaction, based on a comparison between the workplace and prison:

PRISON	*THE WORKPLACE*
You get time off for good behaviour	You get rewarded for good behaviour with more work
They allow your family and friends to visit	You can't even speak to your family and friends
All expenses are paid by taxpayers, with no work required.	You get to pay all the expenses to go to work, and then they deduct taxes from your salary to pay for prisoners
You are supervised by wardens who often turn out to be sadists	You are supervised by managers who often turn out to be sadists

We have looked at ladder-hopping as a way of finding your equilibrium.

But what happens if you still feel dissatisfied? What alternative do you have if the problem is not that you don't want to work for this ladder or that ladder, but that you don't want to work for any ladder?

Apart from perpetual unemployment, your only alternative is to become self-employed, to join the entrepreneurial world.

But what precisely do we mean by the terms entrepreneurship, entrepreneurs and entrepreneurial skills?

It was President George W Bush who was probably misquoted as saying that the French don't have a word for entrepreneur. (Needless to say, this is a French word!)

Yet the same George W showed that he knows a thing or two about entrepreneurship when he told the Small Business Association: "Without entrepreneurs, the American dream would go unrealised."

Often, the definition of entrepreneurship depends on which business guru is doing the defining.

Here are a few of the definitions I have come across over the years:

AN ENTREPRENEUR IS SOMEONE WHO....

- is willing and eager to create a new venture in order to present a concept to the marketplace.
- creates and manages change by pursuing opportunity.
- discovers, evaluates and exploits business opportunities.
- dynamically and innovatively identifies and exploits new opportunities in a wide range of business and organisation contexts.
- acts with passion for a purpose, lives proactively, and leverages resources to create value.
- attempts a new business or creates a new venture.
- is self employed
- expands an existing business organisation.
- pursues business opportunities beyond known resources to create wealth.
- converts ideas into viable business by means of ingenuity, hard work, resilience, imagination and luck.
- starting with nothing more than an idea for a new venture, has the ability to take it to the point at which the business can sustain itself financially.

That's a lot of definitions, isn't it? To simplify things, we will adopt the working definition of entrepreneur that I proposed in *Fire in the Belly:*

Anyone who feels the urge to be their own boss, and who goes out and starts their own business.

It is at this critical point - where you start to seriously consider entrepreneurship as a real option - that you need to ask 10 key questions.

If you can answer these questions to your own satisfaction, you can declare yourself emotionally fit to make the switch from the world of employment to the world of self-employment.

> *I am the kind of guy who kept getting spit out of the corporate world. I don't like wearing ties, I have a problem with authority and I just couldn't fit in anywhere.*
> Copywriter John Carlton

10 KEY QUESTIONS THAT DETERMINE WHETHER YOU'RE FIT TO MAKE THE EMOTIONAL SWITCH FROM EMPLOYEE TO ENTREPRENEUR

QUESTION 1: Dare I leave the security of the employment world?

49 years before the start of the Common Era, the Roman senate ordered Julius Caesar to relinquish control of the armies he had commanded as governor in Gaul.

Caesar retaliated by invading Italy. But when he reached the Rubicon River on the border between Gaul and Italy, he paused before crossing into Roman territory. Uttering the words: 'Jacta alea est' (The die is cast), he eventually overcame his scruples, and led his troops over the river.

Ever since, "crossing the Rubicon" has symbolised the tipping point, the point-of-no-return decision. When you decide that you want to leave the employment world, you are crossing your own personal Rubicon.

Let's recap your entrepreneurial journey so far:

- **You went to school**
- **You got a job**
- **You moved to a better job**
- **You had an AHA! moment, and discovered that you didn't like the employment world (or the employment world didn't like you)**
- **You decided to jump off the employment ladder**

Acknowledging to yourself that you no longer wish to be part of the employment world, is a critical point in your entrepreneurial evolution. It's as if an entrepreneurial virus has entered your immune system, and you are no longer the same person you were before.

The first question you need to ask yourself is whether you are emotionally capable of crossing your Rubicon. Can you cut yourself adrift from the ladder (employment) world? Can you survive without the emotional anchor of an employer? Can you give up the security of a solid job for the uncertainty of being your own boss?

Deciding to work on your own means giving up the security of paid employment – and that's no simple matter. Even some of the most successful start-up founders in history found it hard to go against the prevailing wisdom that being an employee is the norm, while running your own business is an aberration.

CASE STUDY

A year after founding Apple, Steve Wozniak was still a Hewlett Packard employee with no plans to ever leave. Steve Jobs managed to secure some serious venture funding for Apple, on condition that Wozniak quit. But at first, Wozniak refused. He argued that he'd designed both the Apple I and the Apple II while working at HP, and there was no reason why he couldn't continue to hold down a 'proper job' there.

On the other hand, just how secure is the fabled security of paid employment? Not very, judging by the ease with which companies are relocating their operations to whichever part of the globe offers them lower wages or better tax incentives. The old certainties associated with paid employment are proving less and less reliable. We all know people who were happy with their job and happy with their employer, and who woke up one morning to hear (often in the media) that their secure job had vanished.

CASE STUDY

Wanda James had three gold cards, an annual salary over $100,000, and a company car. As regional marketing manager for Avery Dennison, an office products company based in Pasadena, California, she had what many people would regard as a dream job. But she felt she wasn't growing any more, and that she had gone as far as she wanted to go in the corporate world. So Wanda bought the Jamaican Café, a Caribbean-style restaurant in Santa Monica, and turned it into a highly successful business. Looking back on her decision to swap her lucrative job for the unsure waters of entrepreneurship, Wanda says that she never felt that she was giving up anything of any huge importance. Her need to find something more fulfilling in her life was far more important to her than the so-called security of a paid job.

But even if job security is not what it used to be, you still need to ask yourself whether you can live without it.

Can you handle the fact that ladder people often don't understand what motivates the entrepreneur?

Many ladder people are quite antagonistic towards anyone willing to risk their money to follow a dream. They view the entrepreneurial world with suspicion, hostility and jealousy.

Where do these negative views come from?

For some ladder people, this comes from their home upbringing. People whose parents are employees of business or government organisations are more likely to also want to seek a safe and secure job. When they were growing up, these people would have heard discussions at home about pay rises, retirement plans, medical benefits, sick leave, vacation days, and the iniquities of bosses. They would learn to disparage the notion of entrepreneurship, and to be suspicious of excess zeal and industriousness.

It can be very different for children raised in entrepreneurial homes. They are more likely to absorb the cultural norms of their entrepreneurial parents. They are more likely to go it alone. They are likely to hear about the problems that employees can cause. They would listen to money and business being discussed at the dinner table, and they would learn that tax avoidance is a good thing. They may also be used to a parent bringing work home from the office, or a parent working long or irregular hours.

But while children in entrepreneurial families undoubtedly hear entrepreneurial music, and children in non-entrepreneurial families hear non-entrepreneurial music, many ladder children can - and do - become entrepreneurs. And the opposite is also true: many entrepreneurial children can - and do - become employees.

CASE STUDY

Paula and Joe and their 5-year-old daughter Emily moved into a house that was next door to a building plot. Emily was fascinated with all the activity going on next door, and she started chatting with the construction workers. Her parents were happy for her to broaden her horizons, and saw this as an early introduction to the world of solid employment.

The builders adopted Emily. She was always hanging around near the site, and she became the project mascot. They allowed her to sit with them while they had tea and lunch breaks, and gave her little jobs to do to make her feel important. At the end of the first week, they presented her with a pay envelope containing 5 Euro in 50 cent coins.

Emily took her 'pay' home. Her parents suggested that she take the money she had received to the bank the next day to start a savings account. When they got to the bank, Emily explained to the cashier about her 'work' on the building site and the fact she had a 'pay packet'.

"You must have worked very hard to earn all this," said the bank cashier. Emily proudly replied, "I worked all last week with the men building a big house."

"My goodness gracious," said the cashier, "Will you be working on the house again this week?"

Emily thought for a moment, and then she said, "That depends on whether those sh*ts at Chadwicks deliver the f**king bricks."

Basically, Question 1 is about whether you can face the prospect of giving up the four solid legs of the security ladder, in order to stand on your own two feet.

If you're not sure that you can manage this, then maybe you should wait until you are ready. There is no shame in deciding to delay your entry into the entrepreneurial world. There is nothing wrong with biding your time on the ladder until you feel ready to jump off.

No one can make this decision for you. No one else can tell you whether you are ready or not.

> *Leaving nice co-workers, a stable paycheck, and 12 years of tenure with one company was the scariest thing I'd ever done. And yet looking back, it was the defining moment not only of my career, but of my personal development as well. I am now so enamoured of blazing my own trail that I could never go back—I am hopelessly, incurably, unemployable.*
> Michael J. Katz, founder, Blue Penguin Development

If, however, you believe that you can cope with severing the umbilical cord that ties you to the employment world, it's time to ask the next question. Because being primed for jumping off the ladder is not enough. Before you start your own business, something has to trigger your departure from the ladder.

QUESTION 2:
Do I trust the reasons that triggered my decision to go it alone?

The path to entrepreneurship is a multi-faceted interactive process. When exploring your motivation for seeking the entrepreneurial route, you need to examine the factors that triggered your decision to leave the ladder world.

In the course of my work with aspiring entrepreneurs, I have come across many different triggers that influence the decision to leave the so-called comforts of the employment world to become self-employed:

- I need to do my own thing
- I can't wait to be my own boss
- I'm disillusioned with the corporate world
- I become energised when I spot an opportunity
- Bad experiences in the employment world made me vow never to work for someone else again
- The job market is tight and entrepreneurship seems like a better alternative
- I was fired
- I've always been interested in the world of self-employment
- I was born with entrepreneurial genes

- I'm bored with my job
- I always argue with my boss – so I reckon I might as well be my own boss

I find it useful to distinguish between two types of triggers.

1. Push triggers, where the stimulus comes from inside you, and pushes you to embark on the entrepreneurial path.

2. Pull triggers, where something from the outside pulls you towards starting your own business.

Push trigger 1: MONEY TO SPARE

> *The definition of a wealthy man is one whose income is $100 a year higher than his wife's sister's husband.*
> H.L. Mencken

Circumstances can suddenly place a sizeable amount of money at your disposal:

You win the lottery
A great-aunt you never heard of bequeaths you money in her will
You receive a substantial early-retirement handout as part of downsizing
You make a killing on the stock market
Your horse comes in at 500:1

Insufficient funding is often seen as a major reason why businesses fail. So the ability to start out without the need for external financing should be a good thing.

But entrepreneurship is not just about money. It can sometimes be better to be pulled along by a dream, than to be pushed along by a money pot.

CASE STUDY

Jenny could not believe her luck. She had married into a very wealthy family. Her husband's family had a huge house, they took trips and cruises, and the children went to the best private schools. Jenny herself came from much humbler origins. Her father had held the same job for all his working life, and had risen to chief clerk in the Town Hall.

Jenny had done a degree in marketing, and happily accepted her father-in-law's offer to work in the research department of his investment bank. Intoxicated by the vast amounts of money flowing through the bank, Jenny pestered her father-in-law to allow her to join the company's investment department. She actually did well, but she was not satisfied with being under anyone else's control. She persuaded her reluctant father-in-law to give her $2 million in order to set up her own portfolio management company.

Overjoyed with being her own boss, Jenny did what she had seen every boss do. She bought beautiful offices. She hired great-looking staff. She had a great car. She enjoyed long lunches. The one thing she didn't do was devote her efforts to her business. Unsurprisingly, her business folded within a few months. The money had enticed her, but she had no concept of the entrepreneurial mindset needed to start, run and grow a successful business.

Starting a new business just because you have the financial ability to do so is not a good enough reason on its own to leave the employment world.

Beware of this trigger.

Push trigger 2: TRAUMATIC EVENTS

Sometimes, adversity can tip the balance.

CASE STUDY

Although she was at the top of her career, London barrister Polly Higgins could not get rid of a niggling feeling that her work was not addressing the things that were most important to her. Instead of fighting other people's fights, she felt she wanted to turn her energy to fighting for what really mattered to her: the environment. But she did nothing concrete about her plans – until the fateful morning of 7th July 2005, when London was shaken by a series of deadly terrorist bombings. Polly lived just five minutes from Tavistock Square, and the bus explosion there shook the foundations of her home. At some point during the confusing first hours following the explosions, Polly's sister called to see if she was alright. Polly burst into tears, and said: "There has to be a better way. We have to make this a better world, one where people aren't driven to take such terrible action." The events of that awful day triggered Polly's decision to quit her job and to start The Lazy Environmentalist online store.

The following case study shows how trauma of another kind was the stimulus for an entrepreneurial career.

CASE STUDY

Vickie Stringer was from a middle-class Detroit neighbourhood. Her mother was a schoolteacher and her father was an electrical engineer. Vickie dropped out of college, and fell in love with a drug dealer who disappeared after getting her pregnant. She continued to deal drugs, and was making $30,000 a week when she sold a kilo of cocaine to a police informant in Columbus, Ohio.

Vickie was sentenced to 5 years in a federal penitentiary. Three months before she got out of jail, she felt a strong urge to tell her story. Six weeks later, she had a manuscript for a fictionalised story of her life, "Let That Be the Reason." She was a 29-year-old felon with no degree, no résumé, almost no legal work experience, no money, and no prospects. She got a job as a bartender at Columbus Airport, all the while trying to interest publishers in her manuscript.

After she received 26 rejection slips, she decided to self-publish. She raised enough funds from family and friends to print 2,500 copies, and sold her book door-to-door. One of her customers in the airport bar showed the manuscript to UpStream Publications, an African American-owned house based in Brooklyn. UpStream responded with a $50,000 offer, and the book eventually sold over 100,000 copies.

Her second book, "Imagine This," also hit the best seller lists. After a writer named K'wan asked her to publish his book, Gangsta, Vickie decided to start her own publishing company, Triple Crown. Manuscripts started coming in from all over, and she began signing up hip-hop writers and publishing their books. In a few short years, Vickie went from drug queen to owner of a $1.8 million company.

While no one actively seeks traumatic triggers as a stimulus to start a business, there is no doubt that trauma or tragedy can focus the mind, and awaken hitherto dormant entrepreneurial stirrings.

Push trigger 3: DISILLUSIONMENT, FRUSTRATION, UNEASE

Frustration with the ladder world is one of the most frequently cited triggers for self-employment.

Individuals who are dissatisfied with their jobs appear to be more likely to seek entrepreneurial activity.

> *I exchanged the ill-tempered atmosphere of the corporate finance department for the sweet air of a book-lined study overlooking my garden. I was in control of what I was doing in a way that I had never been during my 15-year office career. I no longer felt a little older each day.*
> Martin Vander Weyer

This sense of unease, disillusionment and frustration has practical, emotional/philosophical and authority related roots.

Practical factors include the working conditions and prospects of the employment world:

- **You are not happy with your slow progress up the promotional ladder**
- **You are fed up with the long commute to work**
- **You are frustrated by the slow pace of organisational change**
- **You are uncomfortable with the constant threat of redundancy**
- **You object when others take credit for your ideas, and when you are blamed for the mistakes of others**
- **You want to work the hours that suit your individual body clock**
- **You dislike the office politics**
- **You resent making money for someone else**

Emotional/philosophical factors are about the feeling that despite your credentials and qualifications, the actual experience of employment is soulless. When you want to be a participant rather than an observer, you won't be satisfied with the ordinary.

- You are not fulfilled at work, and you want to make your own unique contribution
- You feel trapped, with no room for personal growth
- You find precious little motivation to go to work.
- You find your work boring and mindless, and you are frustrated at not being able to express your creativity
- You are fed up with hearing more "but" than "wow"
- You want something more spiritually rewarding

Authority-related factors are all about a feeling that you are not in control of your life. You don't like others having control over your actions. You feel like you're back at school, needing permission for everything you do. Authority-related factors are about personal autonomy.

- You are impatient with the rules and regulations
- You resent being told what to do by a boss or supervisor, and you do not like being subject to their whims
- You realise that no boss will ever fully appreciate your unique talents
- You want more control over your job stability
- You do not like being nagged to get something done

- You want to be master of your own schedules, agendas, time and pace
- You feel constitutionally unfit to work for anyone else
- You feel unemployable

CASE STUDY

Damon Dash, head of the Roc-A-Fella Records empire, always knew he wanted to be his own boss, and looked up to people like Bill Gates. He got his first job in a deli when he was 14. On the first day, he was told to deliver something. His reaction was: "I'm not taking orders from anyone." After less than an hour in the employment world, Damon had enough and walked out.

Few people have described the disillusionment with the corporate world better than psychoanalyst Corinne Maier, the French civil servant who worked as an economic consultant at Electricité de France – EDF.

Her best-selling book, "Bonjour Paresse" (Hello Laziness – Jumping off the corporate ladder) is part satire and part manifesto for bored and disgruntled corporate workers. She describes corporate culture as the "crystallisation of the stupidity of a group of people at a given moment."

Her book offers tongue-in-cheek "Cover Your Butt" tips about how to navigate the corporate culture, and is packed with subversive techniques for looking productive without actually doing anything:

- **Keep a low profile**: Don't stand out of the crowd. Don't be outspoken, don't volunteer, don't make waves.
- **Don't over perform**: There's no point excelling at your job, it will only make your colleagues resentful. They'll look for ways of tripping you up, because you show them up in a bad light.
- **Don't under perform**: Don't give anyone an excuse to get rid of you. Never do any more or any less than what is expected of you.
- **Don't complain**: It's never a good idea to complain. Management is not interested in your problems or your suggestions. Don't trust a boss who asks "How Are Things?"
- **Don't get involved in office politics**: Stay neutral. Be aware of what's going on, but don't ally yourself with anyone. Your perceived allegiance to the wrong crowd could cost you your job.
- **Don't come into work after the boss**: Management care more about when you arrive than what you do when you're at work. Don't disappoint them
- **Submerge your own personality**: Don't wear your emotions on your sleeve. Smile, get on with it, and don't give anything away. Learn to be a cog in a bigger machine. Be the best cog you can be.
- **Seek out the most useless positions**. The more useless, the more difficult it is to assess your contribution to the firm's assets.
- **Conform:** You will not be judged on the way you do your work, but on your ability to conform.

According to Maier, you can achieve "active disengagement" by mastering your company's jargon, shuffling papers and cultivating a personal network among your colleagues.

Other gems from the book:

- *Since you could be replaced any day of the week by some idiot off the street, do as little work as possible.*
- *Pretence is one of the main activities of business, and only communist regimes have churned out more jargon than modern business.*
- *Once in the middle of a meeting on motivation, I dared to say that the only reason I came to work was to earn my crust: 15 seconds of total silence followed and everyone looked embarrassed.*

The Los Angeles Times called the book "an exhilarating complaint against work," while The Village Voice called it "a graceful attack on the corporate world."

Boredom with the corporate world can be a powerful cause of disillusionment, as the following case study illustrates.

CASE STUDY

When Clint Greenleaf was a student, he wrote a book on business dress and etiquette called "Attention to Detail: A Gentleman's Guide to Professional Appearance and Conduct" as a joke. After college, he went to work at

Deloitte & Touche, but became quickly bored and miserable. After discovering that he could do all his work in four hours a day, he wrote a second edition of his book, and it sold like wildfire. After seven months at Deloitte & Touche, he couldn't take any more. His accidental foray into the publishing world had whetted his appetite, and he left his job to start Greenleaf Publishing that has already published over 700 titles.

Disillusionment drove one post office engineer to embark on his own entrepreneurial journey.

CASE STUDY

Howard Pau arrived in Britain at the age of 17 from China, and by the age of 35, he had a good job as an engineer with the British Post Office. He was happy with his choice of career, and his promotion prospects within the Post Office were looking good. He had never seriously entertained the idea of leaving his job until one fateful day in 1981.

On that day, Howard's supervisor held a retirement party at work after 43 years of service in the Post Office. Management had allowed him to invite 50 colleagues to a going-away party. Howard was one of the 70 people who eventually turned up at the party for the popular supervisor.

The following day, when the supervisor arrived at work, he was presented with a music system as a retirement gift - and a bill for the extra 20 people who had attended the party. Howard was shocked, depressed and disillusioned. He did some soul-searching. "Am I going to wait for my music centre or am I going to make my own destiny?" He realised that he was no longer prepared to be a company man, and he set out in a totally different direction.

Together with his two brothers, he opened Ireland's first store that specialised in supplying Asian foods to restaurants. Today, Howard's Asia Market employs 60 people, and supplies Chinese and Indian restaurants across Ireland. And all because of the mean-spiritedness of the management at the Post Office.

Is disillusionment a good reason to leave the ladder world? There is no simple answer. But you must distinguish between disillusionment with your present employer, and disillusionment with all employers. If all your frustrations are centred on your present boss, you might find another boss who does not generate such strong feelings of revulsion.

> *The unspoken factor behind the entrepreneurial boom is that working for most companies is so demeaning to the human spirit that many talented people are forced out the door.*
> John Naisbitt

Push trigger 4: GETTING FIRED

Getting fired is the mother of all push triggers. When you are fired, you are quite literally pushed off your ladder. There are all sorts of fancy names for getting fired:

> **Being downsized**
> **Being made redundant**
> **Losing your job**
> **Getting canned**
> **Early retirement**
> **Last in first out**
> **Being dismissed**
> **Being let go**
> **Being terminated**

But the bottom line is the same: You are history. One day you can be in a safe, secure job with a blue-chip employer. The next day someone on the other side of the world presses a button – and your job is no longer yours.
"I'll show them!" is a common reaction. "Who do they think they are?" is another.

> *Gill: It was something my boss said to me that persuaded me to start my own business.*
> *Brenda: What was that?*
> *Gill: He said: "You're fired."*

Most of you will have gone through the experience of losing a job in the course of your working career. And whether you lost your job due to genuine cutbacks or because you did not fit in, you must have reacted in some way.

If you have ever been fired, how did you react when you found out?

The chances are that you reacted strongly. Losing your job can be a severe blow to the ego. It's normal to feel very angry, very hurt, and very sorry for yourself. Losing your job can be a powerful motivation for wanting to start your own business.

But the question is: Should you be making big decisions – such as the decision to leave the employment world altogether – at such a vulnerable time?

If you were the passenger in a car driven by someone suffering from Road Rage, you wouldn't trust the driver's reactions.

In the same way, deciding to start your own business as a form of revenge could be misplaced anger. You must question your own motives and reactions when you are suffering from Redundancy Rage.

> *Getting fired is nature's way of telling you that you had the wrong job in the first place.*
> Hal Lancaster

Becoming self-employed can look attractive when you can't find a job. But it is not the only option. You could look for another salaried position. This could be an opportunity – albeit involuntary – for some corrective ladder-hopping.

Above all, you need to be honest with yourself. If your first instinct after being fired is to start out on your own, ask yourself the following questions:

> Is this a knee-jerk reaction?
> Am I acting on the rebound?
> Can I trust my reactions?
> Is anger a good enough justification for starting a new business?
> Do I have a pattern of being fired frequently?
> Did I decide to start my own business in a fit of revenge?
> Did I get fired because I wanted to be fired?
> Am I tempted to start my own business out of desperation or out of excitement?

Sometimes, losing a job can be a blessing in disguise. Some "necessity entrepreneurs" are able to convert their high-octane cocktail of raw emotions into a powerful entrepreneurial pursuit.

CASE STUDY

When Pat Lynch lost his job as finance director of a technology company that collapsed with the loss of 1,400 jobs, he realised that he had three choices. He could relocate to another operation of the same company overseas; he could move to another multinational employer; or he could set up his own business. The first option was unattractive because he had young children. The second option was discarded because he felt it did not offer enough of a challenge.

Believing that he had sufficient experience to successfully launch his own venture, he chose the entrepreneurial option. Using his redundancy money and a grant from a local enterprise agency, Pat established Microtech Cleanroom Services, which is in the business of cleaning and supplying garments for the cleanroom sector. Lynch's customers for his antistatic protection, garment laundry and supply, laundering of disposable products and locker supply services included IBM and Boson Scientific. Within three years, Lynch sold a majority holding to Ireland's leading linen supply company, National Linen Ltd, and promptly invested most of it in another start-up.

CASE STUDY

After graduating in aerospace engineering from Ryerson University, Avinash Singh became a global project manager for the IT department of Sapient Corp., a business consulting and technology services firm. He enjoyed working for a company that had a very strategic IT outlook, and a strong focus on long-term strategies. But when Sapient decided to move its internal IT operations into fire-fighting mode, Singh decided this was not the direction he wanted to go. He accepted a generous severance package, and examined his options. He could have easily hopped back into the job stream again, and indeed he received several job offers. But going back to being an IT manager just didn't feel right. As an employee, he had always felt a sense of detachment. As much as he wanted to contribute, the fact that he had no part in the ownership bothered him.

So Singh decided to use his severance pay as the golden parachute that could help him realize the dream of owning his own business. He started his own IT infrastructure services company, Relevate, that targets the neglected market of small and medium businesses. Although he traded his 50-hour work week for a 100-hour one, Singh feels a much greater sense of fulfilment than he ever felt as an employee.

Many people turning to entrepreneurship are corporate refugees who have been pushed rather than pulled into their new ventures by joblessness, or by the fear of being made redundant.

It can make perfect sense to start your own business as a reaction to being fired. But deciding to leave the ladder world completely just because you were fired is not the only option. Your best course is to honestly monitor your motivations.

Pull Trigger 1: THE PROSPECT OF MAKING LOTS OF MONEY

Now it's time to examine some pull triggers.

Earlier, we explored what happens when the availability of money becomes a push trigger. But the prospect of making a pile of money can also be a powerful pull trigger. There are many employees who understandably resent the fact that they are toiling in order to make money for someone else.

> *When I turned 30, my life was going nowhere and I was tired of using the art of trying to make someone else rich, so I went out on my own.*
> Copywriter John Carlton

Desire for autonomy and control consistently outranks wealth in surveys that explore the complex motivations of people who start businesses. According to the National Federation of Small Business Owners, less than 20% of the current business owners started a business for money.

In Canada, the average self-employed male works 49.6 hours per week (over 9 hours more than employed males), 51.4 weeks a year (about 5 weeks more than employed males). For this added work, the Canadian male makes about $4,000 less in earnings per year than his employed counterpart.

But for most aspiring entrepreneurs, it is a myth that money is the main trigger. Only a handful of the thousands of people who have attended my Do I Have What It Takes? seminars claim that they are attracted by the vast amount of money they stand to earn as entrepreneurs.

The lure of money alone is not a reliable trigger. You have to really want to be your own boss, you have to be prepared for hard work, if you take the entrepreneurial route. Looking for a fast track to a fast buck is not wise.

Don't get me wrong. I would love to see you driving a 4x4 BMW. I would love to see you buy a magnificent house, and set yourself and your family up in a life of luxury. I hope you make it. It's just that the lure of money alone is not a safe enough trigger to start your own business.

In other words, high earnings should be the benefit of achieving your goal of working for yourself, not the goal itself.

> *I had no ambition to make a fortune.*
> *Mere money-making has never been my goal, I had an ambition to build.*
> John D. Rockefeller

Pull Trigger 2: AN OPPORTUNITY BECKONS

The classic pull trigger is when you spot an opportunity. You feel that an opportunity is beckoning you. Something out there is pulling you off the employment ladder. You are overwhelmed with a conviction that you can do something with this opportunity.

- Have you ever had an idea, and wondered why no one else had thought of it before?
- Have you ever seen a business opportunity that had your name on it?
- Have you ever had an idea about which you did nothing and then regretted the lost opportunity?
- Have you ever had an idea, and then watched helplessly as someone else made something of it?

> *Entrepreneurs are simply those who understand that there is little difference between obstacle and opportunity - and are able to turn both to their advantage.*
> Niccolo Machiavelli

It's often been said that 100 people can be looking at the same wall, but it is only the entrepreneur who sees a door. Well, it's true. Opportunities can jump out at you, even if no one else sees them.

CASE STUDY

George Colony is one of the most influential leaders in the world of technology. As founder and CEO of Forrester Research, his analysis has been quoted in The Wall Street Journal, The London Times and The Economist, and he has featured on CNN, CNBC, and National Public Radio.

Colony's rise to global fame started just after he graduated from Harvard. He looked at the IT field, and believed that he had spotted an opportunity that others had not yet grasped.

Convinced that there was a much bigger potential in the PC than the market had realised, Colony launched Forrester Research in the basement of his home in Cambridge, Mass. He published Forrester's first report, "The Professional Automation Report," in 1983.

Immediately afterwards he signed up IBM as Forrester's first client, and signed up NEC as Forrester's first client that did not have its corporate head office in the USA. Forrester has never looked back, and has consistently been at the forefront of technological advances.

We often miss opportunities, screen them out, or discount them, because they don't fit into our current goals or strategy. The trick is to always be alert to opportunities, and to act on them when you spot them.

> *I was seldom able to see an opportunity until it ceased to be one.*
> Mark Twain

Ask yourself:

- What opportunities are there in my work environment?
- What can I see that customers want that they are not receiving?
- How can I improve the products or services that I see around me?
- What product or service already exists elsewhere but not in my local market?
- How can I turn my talents, my hobbies, my proven track record into the basis of a profitable business?

The idea for a new business can hit you in the most unlikely places.

CASE STUDY

Gary Klein was working for a New York shipper when toothache sent him to his dentist. As he sat in the waiting room, he noticed an aquarium. As someone who kept several fish tanks at home, Gary knew that the dentist's aquarium was in a deplorable state. He also knew exactly what was needed to be done to clean them. Spotting a business opportunity, Gary offered to come and clean the aquarium each month for a small fee. Word soon spread through the dentist's network of colleagues, and soon Gary had dozens of monthly clients. He was encouraged to advertise for new accounts in local professional magazines, and the number of people who wanted their aquariums cleaned reached several hundred a month. Gary gave up his day job, and a brand new business was born.

CASE STUDY

When Tom McGuinness dropped out of college at 21, the last thought on his mind was a career in business. At the time, he believed that to be in business, you either had to be a crook or a cheat. So he left Ireland and went to a poor area of South America where he was to spend the next eight years as a missionary. Tom only returned to Ireland in 1979 after his brother sent him a ticket to allow him to attend his wedding. Once back home, Tom drifted into managing a horse riding school before seeing an opportunity to develop a new type of horse blanket.

One day, he stumbled across a "How to Start Your Own Business" book which he sat up all night reading. The next morning, he decided to start his own horse blanket business. His only piece of equipment was his mother's old redundant sewing machine, which he used to make prototype after prototype until he got it right. Tom's Horseware company went on to transform the entire market sector, and the business now exports all over the world.

Many people start a business because their ideas have been rejected by their employers.

CASE STUDY

Rachael Lewis worked as a receptionist/messenger for an adult modelling agency in Miami. Bored with simply answering the phones, she started thinking about ways that the agency could expand. Rachael came up with the idea of developing a kids division. She took her plan to the owners of the agency, and offered to run the proposed new kids division. They said it was not a good idea. So she left to found Rachael's Totz 'n' Teenz Model Management Inc., which she ran from her Manhattan apartment. Her agency now works with over 150 teen models, many of whom have signed contracts with the likes of Ralph Lauren, Tommy Hilfiger, Avon, and Toys 'R' Us.

CASE STUDY

Bernard Coyle used to return at the end of his bread round with empty trays of crumbs. More and more customers were asking him for the breadcrumbs that gathered on the trays. So instead of throwing the breadcrumbs out, Bernard kept them for these customers, who used the crumbs as the base ingredient of stuffings for roasts and other dishes. Bernard's first instinct was to suggest to his employer that he should use this opportunity for making additional revenue stream by systematically collecting the crumbs and selling them. When the management displayed no interest in Bernard's idea, he left the business and set up his own dedicated breadcrumbs business, The Crumb Factory. Under the Mr. Crumb brand, Bernard now offers breadcrumbs, gourmet stuffings, fresh crust toppings and dessert puddings. In February 2005, The Crumb Factory won Ireland's National Small Business Award.

CASE STUDY

After leaving university, Imogen Roberts worked briefly in sales for a software company, but she discovered very quickly that she wanted the freedom to control her own work. She spotted her entrepreneurial opportunity while planning a holiday to Cuba in November. Surprisingly, she discovered that very few retail outlets catered for the growing all-year-round jet-set lifestyle. Imogen saw a gap in the market, and at the age of 23, she established the Claudia Strand online retail store.

Any trigger, push or pull, is a healthy trigger if you were already looking for an excuse to leave the employee world.

And notwithstanding my health warnings about certain triggers, almost any trigger will be appropriate if you are emotionally ready to switch gears to self-employment.

Once you are satisfied that you can trust your trigger, it's time to move on to the next question.

> *You are the only warden over your mind. You hold the keys that can free your mind to see all of the opportunities out there.*
> Dave Hertner

QUESTION 3: Can I cope with the reaction of my family?

Ah, the family, bless them.

It is human nature that once you feel the urge to join the world of self-employment, you want to share the good news with your loved ones.

♦ Husband	♦ Boy/girlfriend
♦ Wife	♦ Best friend
♦ Partner	♦ Uncle
♦ Fiancé	♦ Aunt
♦ Fiancée	♦ Cousin
♦ Parent	♦ Grandparent
♦ Child	♦ Other family members

Family and close friends certainly play a critical role in your entrepreneurial odyssey. However, the nature of that role is often grossly misunderstood.

If you consult the vast majority of experts, gurus, books and websites offering advice on the subject, these are the kind of comments you are likely to find:

- *Families must create a very supportive home atmosphere for entrepreneurs*
- *Starting a new business has more chance of succeeding when this is a family decision*
- *Unless you have emotional support from your family, your new business is doomed.*
- *While family and friends may not be able to relate to your specific fears about starting a business, you must be able to count on them for emotional support.*
- *You can't walk the start-up tightrope without the support of loved ones to steer you in the right direction.*
- *Without the backing of family, you are not firing on all pistons.*

A leading national enterprise support agency states categorically in a handbook for aspiring entrepreneurs:

> *"We'd go so far as to say that you shouldn't even consider the possibility of starting a business unless your family wholeheartedly supports your decision to start a business."*

Let's assume for a moment that the experts are right. Let's assume that you have experienced an entrepreneurial epiphany. Let's assume that you want to share the good news, and you come bouncing home to announce to your family or friends that you have decided to give up your salaried position in order to start your own business.

It's only natural that you expect to receive their blessing.

After all, haven't the experts assured you that your family will be supportive? So when you are about to deliver your "entrepreneurial announcement," you expect praise for your initiative.

I prefaced my book, *My Family Doesn't Understand Me*, with the following updated version of the classic Fairy Tale, *The Three Bears:*

> *Once upon a time, in a place called Honeytown, there lived three bears: Daddy Bear, Mummy Bear and Baby Bear.*
>
> *Daddy Bear worked as a security guard in the local branch of First National Honey Bank. Mummy Bear was a supervisor at the Honeytown glass jar company. Baby Bear was minded by Grandma and Grandpa Bear.*
>
> *Daddy Bear was very good at his job, and frequently made suggestions to management on how they could tighten up security at the bank. But from an early age, Daddy Bear had always had a bee in his bonnet. An entrepreneurial bee. He had always liked the idea of being his own boss, and was forever on the lookout for a suitable opportunity.*
>
> *One day as he was browsing through the Honeytown Times, he read a report that Bruinbank, Paddington Bank and Rupert Bank were all planning to open branches in*

Honeytown in the near future.

Daddy Bear's entrepreneurial wheels started turning. "This is my chance", he thought to himself. "I have become extremely knowledgeable in the area of bank security. I've always wanted to do my own thing. Why don't I use my expertise, and set up my own bank security consultancy business, offering my services to the new banks?"

Bursting with excitement and energy, Daddy Bear went bouncing home to share his good news with Mummy Bear. "Guess what, honeybunch," he told her, "I've decided to leave my job in the bank, and to become my own boss. I'm going to start my own business as a bank security consultant."

Mummy Bear rushed up to Daddy Bear and almost knocked him over with the force of her loving bear hug. "Oh sweetie", she said. "You're so brave. I always knew you had it in you. I always knew I'd married someone with drive, someone with ambition, someone who knew how to take the initiative. Baby Bear will be so proud to have a daddy who runs his own business."

"And of course, sweetie," Mummy Bear murmured into his ear, "you know you can always count on me for all the emotional support you need, you clever Daddy Bear you."

That evening, Mummy Bear organised an impromptu get-together for all the family to tell them about Daddy Bear's plans. Grandpa Bear slapped Daddy Bear on the

> back as he growled: "Good for you, son." Mummy Bear's sister Bessie Bear heartily congratulated him, and Cousin Beryl Bear slapped a great big kiss on Daddy Bear's cheek.
>
> Delighted, validated and empowered by the enthusiastic response of Mummy Bear and the other members of the Bear family, Daddy Bear gave in his notice at Honeytown Bank. He set up his own bank security business, and was soon running a successful company supplying security services to all the banks in Honeytown and beyond.
>
> Mummy Bear, Daddy Bear and Baby Bear all lived happily ever after.

If you could write your own script, you would want to hear comments such as these:

- Great!
- Well done you.
- I admire your daring.
- I'm with you all the way.
- Congratulations.
- I knew you had it in you.
- I was waiting for the day when you started up on your own.
- How can I help?
- You're brilliant.
- You were never meant to work for someone else.

And indeed, a lucky few individuals (and bears) do indeed receive the overwhelming family support that they seek and crave when they deliver their entrepreneurial announcement. Their expectations are met in full.

If, after your entrepreneurial epiphany, you enjoy a reception like the one Daddy Bear received, you deserve sincere congratulations.

In fact, I suggest you skip the rest of this chapter.

Unfortunately, would-be entrepreneurs who get family support are an endangered species. A very different reality awaits most people who excitedly try to deliver their entrepreneurial announcement to their loved ones.

No matter what the theory says, evidence from the trenches of entrepreneurial endeavour tells us that most people thinking of starting their own business don't get praise or congratulations from their loved ones.

Instead, they are on the receiving end of abuse, disappointment and downright hostility.

In the course of my work, I have spoken to thousands of people about the reactions they received when they informed their family of their intention to start their own business.

I find it useful to divide these reactions into 4 categories.

CATEGORY 1: Questioning your mental health

- Are you mad?
- You've gone soft in the head.
- Have you lost it?
- You're crazy.
- You're out of your mind.
- You're behaving insanely.
- You need your head examined.
- You need a psychiatrist.
- You're emotionally unstable.
- You're having a nervous breakdown.

CATEGORY 2: Outrage

- How dare you!
- You've got some nerve!
- That's preposterous!
- You arrogant bastard/bitch!
- How could you be so irresponsible?
- Who do you think you are!
- What about the mortgage?
- What about the children's education?
- What about our European vacation?

CATEGORY 3: Put-down

- Stop kidding yourself.
- Get real.
- You'll never make it.
- How could you be so stupid.
- What a dumb idea.

- Stop dreaming.
- Typical of you to think only of yourself.
- Why are you so stubborn?
- Is this another bee in your bonnet?
- You don't have a chance of succeeding.
- You don't have what it takes to be your own boss.

CATEGORY 4: Threat/ultimatum

- I categorically forbid you to do this.
- Over my dead body.
- No way.
- That's what you think.
- If you go ahead, I'm outta here.
- Read my lips - no you're not.

Do any of these sound familiar? Your first reaction when your family and friends respond this way is shock, followed closely by disappointment.

This is perfectly understandable. You ask yourself: "Why did this happen? Can all the experts have got it so wrong?"

Sadly, the answer is yes. Far too many experts perpetuate the myth that family support is automatic, there for the asking. Far too many entrepreneurial support and training organisations still maintain that buy-in from family is a pre-condition for the success of your enterprise.

So what is going on here? Why is on-tap universal emotional support from family and friends not automatically forthcoming?

I believe that the answer is not that your loved ones are bad or sad. It's not that they don't **want** to support you. It's because they are **incapable** of giving the emotional support that aspiring entrepreneurs expect.

The key lies in the fact that most of your loved ones are ladder people!

> *My family believed my business would never work because of the amount of competition. They basically wrote me off, saying that since I was educated, I should be working in a merchant bank.*
> Karan Bilimoria, founder, Cobra Beer

They live in a different world. They have different values. So the more you are lulled into believing that emotional support from family is your right, the more disappointed and shocked you are when you encounter the negativity and hostility.

I found the following posted on an Indian chat room: "For as long as I can remember I have always wanted to be an entrepreneur. The problem was that no one in my middle-class Indian family had ever been a businessman. The entire environment was discouraging. Business is not for you, is the mantra I heard growing up. Get security. Get a job, preferably a secure government job. Don't take risks. These messages get into one's psyche."

Paulo Coellio is the Brazilian writer who is the world's second best-selling authour after John Grisham. His parents thought his dream of becoming a writer was so crazy that they actually committed him to a mental hospital. When Joan Rivers told her parents that she wanted to go into show business, her father too threatened to have her committed.

My own experience was not too different. When I first announced that I wanted to start my own business, some members of my family wanted to bring in the white coats. Clearly I was going through an early mid-life crisis, and I needed urgent counselling.

Most families are incapable of delivering the level of support that their entrepreneurial loved ones crave, because they don't understand the language of entrepreneurship.

As soon as you start thinking about entering the world of self-employment, you start using a new vocabulary, a new shorthand of ideas. It's as if you wake up one morning suddenly able to speak Entreprenese.

You won't find this new language on the curriculum of language schools like Berlitz. You won't find phrase books on "Teach yourself Entreprenese in 7 days."

That's because Entreprenese is a language that you pick up automatically. And critically, it's a language that your family can't speak or understand. When you deliver your entrepreneurial announcement, they look at you as if you are speaking Chinese or ancient Greek.

Look at it from their perspective. You come home all excited, dying to share your good news. And what exactly is it you are sharing with them? That you intend to give up the security of a regular salary in order to go out on your own.

Of course they look at you through a fog of disbelief and incomprehension. Of course they don't understand you. Of course they feel threatened. Of course they panic. Everything you have to say on the subject – is interpreted very differently by them.

Justin attended one of my *Do You Have What It Takes* seminars. I noticed him listening very attentively, and I saw a sense of relief cross his face when I described the disparity between what we want to hear from our family and what we actually hear. That same evening, Justin sent me the following anguished email:

CASE STUDY

I have had a successful career in banking. I'm 35, and I'm good at what I do. I have risen speedily up the corporate ladder, but now I have ants in my pants. I'm ready for something else. I feel that I owe it to myself to try my hand at starting my own business. Like most people in this situation, I probably lulled myself into believing that those close to me – my fiancée Eileen in particular – would rejoice in my plans. I assumed that they would be happy that I was seeking self-fulfilment in the entrepreneurial world.

I also assumed that because Eileen's parents ran a business, they would be supportive too. Boy, was I in for a shock – which is why I could identify with the hostile reactions you spelled out in your seminar. When I got over my initial shock at their reactions, I decided to adopt a conciliatory tone. I thought to myself: you're an intelligent guy. You just need to explain to them what you're doing and why, and they will come around. So I patiently explained the outline of my business plan to Eileen. But the more I explained, the more strident she became. And instead of being able to enlist the support of her parents in my quest to win her over, they turned up the pressure on me even more.

It was at this delicate stage in the proceedings that I attended your seminar today. For the first time since I decided to go solo, I heard words of encouragement. For the first time since I started telling those close to me about my plans, I felt that there's someone who understands me. For the first time, I realised that hostility was the norm, not the exception.

Not unnaturally, I left your seminar feeling validated and empowered. I was more determined than ever to press on with my entrepreneurial plans. I was also intending to explain to Eileen what I had learned about the built-in conflict that you described. I never got the chance. As I got through the door, Eileen issued an ultimatum: "Either you drop your ridiculous entrepreneurial plans, or we are through."

I still love her, but this whole episode has seriously dented my certainty that we can make it as a couple. I do not appreciate ultimatums. I do not appreciate pressure. My entrepreneurial plans were hatched in the hope that we would both benefit from my going it alone, and that we would both be in this together. I never asked to have to make a stark choice, but now that I am being forced to choose, my inclination is to choose my freedom rather than to buckle under and accept someone else's definition of my future happiness."

Often, people in Justin's situation believe that there is something wrong with the way they present their entrepreneurial dreams to their families. I have been asked by many aspiring entrepreneurs: "If I'd handled it differently, if I'd said the right thing, would my loved ones have reacted differently?"

I'm afraid the answer is probably no. There is often no "right" way of breaking the entrepreneurial news. Many families and friends simply cannot respond to the entrepreneurial announcement with the level of enthusiasm you expect. And the more you go into detail, the more alarmed they can become.

The big question for you is: Can you live with that? Can you proceed with your dreams and your plans, even if your family are not 100% - or even 1% - behind you?

If you cannot face the prospect of family disapproval, you may have to shelve your entrepreneurial plans.

If you can proceed with your plans, chapter 5 will offer some thoughts on who you can turn to for support. In the meanwhile, it's time to ask the next question.

QUESTION 4:
Do I understand the difference in mindset between the world of employment and the world of self-employment?

We all go through the school system. And because schools train, condition and brainwash you to become an employee, you now need debriefing, debugging and deprogramming.

Why deprogramming? Because there is a very stark difference between the ladder world and the non-ladder world. The transition from one world to the other can involve genuine culture shock.

In his groundbreaking 1983 paper, "A Perspective on Entrepreneurship," Harvard Business School professor Howard H. Stevenson defined the differences between the employee mindset and the entrepreneur mindset. Employees, said Stevenson, are resource-oriented, while entrepreneurs are opportunity-oriented. The employee mindset person says, "I would love to start my own business, but I don't have the money." Faced with a similar situation, the entrepreneur mindset person says: "Let's start the business and we can finance the business from the cash flow."

> *Entrepreneurship is as much about a mindset as it is about business models and planning.*
> Jeff Zbar

Being self-employed is fundamentally different than being an employee. The distinction between work time and personal time blurs. If a problem arises with the business, it's your problem, and it won't go away merely because you've closed the doors for the day. Decisions you make regarding the business will have a direct and immediate impact on your personal life. Even if you're not operating an internet business, you're basically on call 24 hours a day in the event an emergency arises regarding your business.

> *We are designed, weaned, trained from Day 1 to be productive members of society. And we are heavily guilted into believing that must involve some sort of droning repetitive pod-like dress-coded work for a larger corporate cause.*
> Mark Morford

It's like railway lines. In the bad old days, different European countries had different railway gauges. Any train that tried to travel from a narrow gauge railway on to a wider gauge railway (or vice versa) would inevitably become derailed.

If you want to avoid getting derailed as you move from the ladder world to the self-employment world, you have to urgently find a way of reprogramming your system to the new gauge.

For example, as an employee, other people told you what to do. You were used to having your actions directed by others. But when you run your own business, you have to direct your own actions. There is no point waiting for someone to drop work on your desk or point out what needs to be done – because it won't happen. If you have been an employee for a long time, you will need a heavy dose of deprogramming to cure you of your former attitudes.

Another area where it is critical to deprogram yourself is your relationship to the dimension we call time. There is a fundamental difference in the way employees and self-employed people relate to time. Many salaried employees continue to draw their monthly salary, even when they spend much of the day doing non-work related tasks and playing games on the computer. Any entrepreneur tempted to follow this pattern is doomed to fail.

When you were a salaried employee, you fitted your time input to corporate demands. Essentially, you did what your boss wanted you to do. But as an entrepreneur, time management is self-driven. You need to set your own time. You're the one who dictates the day's schedule. You're the one who decides what needs to be accomplished during the day.

As a salaried employee, you work for specified periods in a specified location. This allows you to focus your time and efforts on accomplishing your work assignments without being encumbered by the demands at home. But as an entrepreneur, you have no one to tell you where and when to work. There is a thinner line between home and work, and demands between the two can overlap.

In other words, employees tend to make their schedules fit the clock, while entrepreneurs tend to make the clock fit their schedules.

To illustrate this, imagine that during the course of a working day in your ladder job, you look at your watch (we're talking about the old-fashioned watches, not the digital ones.) What do you see?

Well, I'll tell you what you don't see. You don't see a clock-face with 12 equidistant numerals. Because every time you look at your watch while you're at work, what you see is in relation to the distance between 9 and 5. You never look at your watch in neutral mode. You never say to yourself: "Oh, how interesting, the time is 10.44 am." The time that you see on your watch is always relative to how long has elapsed since you arrived at work, and how long before the next coffee break, lunch break, or clocking out time at the end of the day.

If it is indeed 10.44, you probably make a mental note that it's 16 minutes to the 11.00 coffee break. If it's 12.44, you know it's soon time for lunch. If it's 16.44, you are already on a countdown to clocking out. If it's after 18.00, you are wondering why you're not home yet - or you're busy calculating your overtime pay.

When you are in someone else's employ, it is almost inevitable that time becomes a function of your agreed working hours.

Now let's consider the clock-face on the entrepreneur's watch.

When you work for yourself, time has a very different value. For the entrepreneur, time is the enemy, because you are always trying to squeeze more than 24 hours into your day. When you look at your watch, you don't see 12 equidistant numerals. What you see is a jumble of deadlines, a queue of competing priorities waiting to be attended to.

When you run your own business, there is always something else that needs urgent attention. There is always something else that should have been completed by now.

- **You should have made an urgent call to your customer**
- **You should have placed an urgent order with a supplier**
- **You should have been to the bank**
- **You should have chased up money you were owed**
- **You should have completed a delivery**
- **You should have sent your tax returns to your accountant**
- **You should have proofread your self-promotion brochure**
- **You should have attended a Chamber of Commerce meeting**
- **You should have ……..**

In other words, every time a self-employed person looks at a watch, <u>**it is always the wrong time!**</u>

This difference in attitude between employees and entrepreneurs is crucial. When you make the switch from employee to self-employed, you need to leave your old watch behind in your place of work, and buy a new watch for your entrepreneurial adventure.

> *It's not the hours you put in your work that counts, it's the work you put in the hours.*
> Sam Ewing

There is another fundamental difference in the way that employees and self-employed relate to time. Most employees have been programmed to believe that they have to trade time for money. They are paid for turning up. When they have done their hours, they go home.

In the world of self-employment, it soon becomes apparent that clients aren't really interested in how long it takes to manufacture a product or to deliver a service. What clients care about is value.

For example, does the value of this book depend on how long it took me to write it? My first book *Fire in the Belly – exploring the entrepreneurial mindset,* took me 4 weeks to write. *Chutzpah – unlocking the maverick mindset of success* took me 4 years. Does that mean I should charge 50 times more for *Chutzpah* than for *Fire in the Belly?* Of course not. As an entrepreneur, you need to de-couple your value from your time.

Now let's look at the different attitudes to pace. Many employees admit to entertaining some of the following thoughts:

- Urgency is relative - tomorrow is another day.
- Why bust a gut for a boss who wouldn't bust a gut for me?
- What's the worse that can happen if I don't finish this today?
- If I complete this task too quickly, I could get my colleagues into trouble.
- If I complete this task too quickly, I may be setting a dangerous precedent for myself in the future.

This colours your attitude to the workplace.

Exercise

- Take a piece of elastic or anything that can stretch.
- Hold the elastic about 6 inches apart in your two hands.
- This represents the size of the assignment you have been given to do.
- Now start pulling your hands apart.
- The elastic stretching further and further represents time.
- The further you stretch the elastic, the more time elapses.
- You stretch the elastic (time) as far as you can without being caught.

This might sound a bit exaggerated, but it serves as a useful model for how employees relate to work.

When you work for someone else, of course you can be loyal and you can be dedicated.

But ultimately your commitment to your employer falls short of fanatical. When push comes to shove, you are dispensable.

If times get tough for your boss, your position is vulnerable. Your loyalty and dedication will be of little use if you lose your job.

But when that loyalty and dedication are placed at the disposal of your own business, the situation is very different:

Exercise:

- Take a large cushion, or piece of sponge.
- Hold it between your two hands.
- This represents the size of the assignment you have to complete.
- Now start pushing your hands together.
- The cushion or foam being squashed represents time.
- The closer you squash the cushion, the less time elapses.
- You condense the time taken to complete the assignment as much as possible – because you have something else urgent to complete immediately after that.

Can you see the difference in attitude? When you own your own business, your work ethic knows no bounds. You are totally committed to your enterprise.

CASE STUDY

Janice was a freelance copywriter who had been brought in by a client to write a 100-page website Help Desk. She was given a desk, a computer, and a list of jobs to complete. It had been years since she had sat a full day in an office, and she had forgotten what office life can be like.

Janice could not believe how much energy was spent in discussing where to eat and what social activities would be undertaken that evening. She was shocked at how much time the team took off at lunch. She was used to cramming as much work into as short a time frame as possible. She was not used to the very different pace of a ladder office. And she totally resented being told by her new colleagues to take her foot off the accelerator. One of them explained: "You're making the rest of us look bad."

Running your own business, especially in the early months, means learning to juggle. You must become a multi-tasker. You need to wear multiple hats and do everything from product development to marketing to record keeping within a 24-hour day period. You will find yourself having to perform almost every work role in your business.

CHECKLIST OF DIFFERENT ROLES YOU PERFORM WHEN YOU RUN YOUR OWN BUSINESS

- CEO/Managing Director/Assistant to the CEO
- Receptionist
- Sales Manager
- Marketing Director
- Advertising Manager
- Financial Director
- Office Manager
- Personnel Manager
- Customer Support Manager
- Recruitment Officer
- Payroll Clerk
- Company Spokesman
- Head of PR
- IT Manager
- Production Manager
- Warehouse Manager
- Complaints Manager
- Safety Manager
- R&D Manager
- Chief Buyer
- Strategist
- Business Manager
- New Business Manager
- Training Manager
- Property Manager
- Janitor
- Handyman
- Catering Manager
- Maintenance Manager

One of the challenges – and part of the fun – of being your own boss is that you learn to cope with multiple roles.

In the ladder world, your roles and responsibilities were often highly defined. Once you work for yourself, you can forget the niceties of role definitions.

CASE STUDY

Linda was a young businesswoman who had just started her own firm. She had rented beautiful offices and furnished them with antiques to create the right ambience. As she sat behind her desk on the first morning, she saw someone enter the outer office. Wishing to appear the hot shot businesswoman, Linda picked up the phone and pretended to be negotiating a major deal. Finally she hung up and asked the visitor "Can I help you?" The man said, "Yeah, I've come to activate your phone lines."

In this chapter, we looked at the change in mindset that is required when making the switch from the ladder world to the world of self-employment.

In the next chapter, we ask how prepared you are for the downside of being your own boss.

Running a start-up company is like being a juggler with a thousand different balls in the air. You can't let any of them drop.
Michael Stern, cofounder, Aquarium Ventures

QUESTION 5:
Am I prepared for the downside of self-employment?

When you contemplate the idea of running your own business, it's easy to imagine the benefits.

For example, isn't it great that no one can turn round and fire you? Never again will you have to suffer the indignity and insult of hearing those dreaded words "You're the weakest link. Goodbye." Never again will you hear the phrase made famous by Donald Trump and Sir Alan Sugar in the US and UK versions of the TV show, The Apprentice: "You're fired."

Another obvious benefit of starting and running your own business is freedom of choice. This can be a very exhilarating experience.

Suddenly, you're the one who dictates the priorities. You call the shots. There is no longer anyone else telling you what to do and when to do it. You're the one who has to balance the competing demands of clients, suppliers, the bank and other stakeholders.

> *It is our choices, Harry, that show what we truly are, far more than our ambitions.*
> Professor Albus Dumbledore to Harry Potter

One way in which you can exercise your freedom of choice is to decide on the character and personality of your business:

- You decide on the name of the company
- You decide on your logo
- You choose your letterheads
- You choose your marketing messages
- You decide what kind of website to have
- You decide on the décor of your office and business premises
- You decide on the equipment and furnishings
- You decide how to fill your schedule.
- You decide which meetings to attend.

Another area of choice concerns the people you work with. The smart entrepreneur chooses to work with people who brighten up the day, not people who cast a shadow over it. When it comes to your own business, you cannot afford to work with anyone who is not on your side, whether inside or outside your company.

- **You decide on whether to employ staff**
- **You choose the people who will work for you**
- **You no longer have to put up with a rude and arrogant client**
- **You no longer have to work with an unpleasant or unreliable supplier**
- **You no longer have to accept the ineptitude of a colleague whom you did not choose**
- **You no longer have to work alongside a nasty colleague**
- **You no longer have to accept the whims of a bullying boss**

You get to decide where you work:

- **You decide whether you want to buy or rent your own premises**

- **You decide whether you want to work closer to home**
- **You decide whether you want to work at home** *(see Question 8)*

You get to choose your own work-life balance:

- **You decide how much time to devote to your family**
- **You decide how much time to devote to your business**
- **You decide how much time to devote to your leisure pursuits**

Looking forward to the upside of the entrepreneurial lifestyle is a pleasurable past-time. But if you want a reality-based foretaste of the entrepreneurial experience, you also need to know about some of the problems you are likely to encounter when you become your own boss.

Cash flow can be a problem. Instead of a stable cash-flow that you enjoyed as a salaried employee, you will now have to face a cash flow that can fluctuate on a daily basis. You may well discover a reluctance to pay for your work.

Some of the excuses you might hear:

- **We didn't receive the invoice**
- **We wish to query an item on the invoice**
- **We didn't receive everything we ordered**
- **There was a problem with the delivery**
- **We're not happy with the product/service**
- **The cheque is in the post**
- **We're having new chequebooks printed**
- **We can't pay you until we are paid by our own client**

In really extreme circumstances, late payment could spell the end of your business. According to the European Commission, 25% of company insolvencies in the EU are the result of late payment.

And if late payment is a problem, non-payment is an even greater problem. If your client becomes insolvent or simply disappears, it doesn't matter how sound your business plan, non-payment could cripple your enterprise. There is also no guarantee that choosing the problematic, costly and time-consuming route of litigation will bring the results you want.

Here are a few things you can do to protect yourself:

- **Studies show that women have greater success at collecting money than men. If you're a man, find a female colleague to nag your client.**
- **Get clients to sign a written contract governing payment and credit terms.**
- **Run a credit-rating check on your client.**
- **Ask for a cash down-payment.**
- **When calling in the debts, be firm but courteous – remember, the money due to you is your money, not the client's money**
- **Don't get personal. "Your company owes our company money" works better than "You owe me money".**
- **Consider the use of invoice-discounting.**
- **Use a debt collection agency as a measure of last resort**

Even your health can be a problem – and many entrepreneurs simply cannot afford to be ill. It wasn't like that when you worked in the ladder world. When you didn't feel well, you got a doctor's note and you stayed at home. Your employer had to survive without you. But when the employer is you, you will genuinely believe that the business cannot survive without you.

Don't be tempted to wish away illness. It's better to take off a couple of days and give your body the rest it needs, than to push your body beyond the limit – and ending up having to take a week off later.

Other downsides of being on your own include the likelihood of finding yourself having to work longer hours than you thought. You will have fewer opportunities to take vacations, you may end up spending more time running the business and less time for those things you really enjoy, and you may have to do unpleasant things such as firing an employee or refusing to hire a friend or relative.

But the area where you are likely to experience the biggest downside is loneliness.

> *Top of mountain great place. But very lonely.*
> Confucius

Study after study in America, Europe and elsewhere identifies loneliness as the biggest problem facing people who start their own businesses. No matter how big or how small your business, the sense of isolation seems to present a formidable psychological as well as professional challenge.

Being an entrepreneur is a lonely occupation, and you have to be emotionally prepared to feel isolated as you build your business. In the run-up to opening your new venture, you will be busy getting everything in place for the launch date. There's too much going for you to feel lonely. But once the business is up and running, you can suddenly feel very alone. You are no longer part of a team, and you no longer receive validation from others.

The root cause of the entrepreneur's sense of isolation is that your normal support systems have deserted you.

As a member of the ladder world, you know that when you have a problem, you can automatically turn to two solid sources of support: your work colleagues and your family.

For example, you can pour your heart out to your work colleagues, your supervisor, team members or even your boss. Often, you can expect to find a sympathetic shoulder to cry on.

And if your colleagues fail to be sympathetic, you can always go home and share your problems with your loved ones. They too can be expected to be sympathetic.

But when you run your own business, you can no longer automatically rely on these two support systems.

> *You are on your own and nobody supports you because it's hard for them to see what you see, and feel the excitement that you feel.*
> Colin Wahl, co-founder, InvestorForce

Let's say you have a problem at work in your new business. Your automatic response might be to share this problem with former work colleagues. So you arrange to meet them after work. After exchanging pleasantries, you start explaining your problem.

Just watch as their eyes glaze over. They won't want to know. They won't understand the world of self-employment, and they won't understand why you deserted them to go out on your own. You realise that you can no longer expect much understanding from that particular support system.

You won't fare much better at home. In the previous chapter, we saw how your family probably reacted to your decision to leave the security of the workplace to start your own business. It is not difficult to imagine the reception you are likely to receive from your loved one when you announce that the customer cheque you deposited yesterday and that covers the mortgage payments and other standing orders, has bounced.

The loss of these two solid support systems is the main cause of the isolation experienced by almost everyone who starts a new business.

Another aspect of loneliness is the realisation that you – and you alone - now bear the ultimate responsibility for your business. This next case study comes from the employment world, but it illustrates the meaning of ultimate responsibility.

CASE STUDY

Ben Sliney was an air traffic controller who had taken a career break of several years to practise law. On September 11th, 2001, Ben turned up for his first day at work as the newly appointed Federal Aviation Administration (FAA) national operations manager in Herndon, Virginia. Within a couple of hours on his first day back, terrorists had hijacked several commercial airliners. But instead of the usual *pattern, where hijackers threaten the pilots and demand that they direct the flight to a different destination, these terrorists had murdered the pilots. The airliners were being used as missiles aimed at strategic targets in the very heart of the USA.*

Faced with a situation that had never occurred in the history of the FAA, Sliney issued the Full Goundstop order, which prevents all commercial or private flights in the country from taking off. No one had ever given this order before. And a little later, Sliney issued a second historic order: every single commercial and private aircraft in the air was to land, regardless of destination.

And all this happened on Sliney's first day back at work. That's taking responsibility. That's a new definition of "The buck stops here."

So how do you compensate for the loneliness of the long distance entrepreneur? We've already seen that friends who are employees have no experience of starting a business. The obvious source of support for the lonely entrepreneur - is another entrepreneur who knows exactly what you are going through.

- **Only another entrepreneur really understand what it's like in the trenches of entrepreneurial effort.**
- **Find Phone A Friend entrepreneurs to turn to when you want honest feedback.**
- **You can freely complain about clients, suppliers, the tax authorities and the bank.**
- **You can swap horror stories about lack of family support.**

- You can receive congratulations when you secure a significant order.
- You can receive consolation when business is lousy.
- You can get reassurance that it's normal to worry about your business.

CASE STUDY

Richard Steward founded Mindbench, a management consultancy, and within two months, the company had four people working on projects. The company could also draw on the services of a network of other freelance consultants. Because Mindbench could not afford offices, everyone worked from home.

Although MS Messenger and Webcams helped them solve technical communications issues, Richard saw that there was no real substitute for the kind of direct human interaction that you can achieve in an office. He realised that it was lonely working all day from home. He found it difficult to keep everyone motivated. He had to grapple with the challenge of keeping confidence levels up, while trying to build a team culture for his bunch of freelancers.

Richard decided that everyone needed to meet up on a regular basis. He was friends with several other home-based entrepreneurs in the early stages of building their own businesses, and he knew that they were all facing similar issues. So he created a semi-formal network to boost everyone's energy levels, to connect, and to use the opportunity to network and share contacts.

The Monday Club meets on the first Monday evening of every month in a restaurant. This self-financing club is all about having fun with other like-minded entrepreneurial people. The idea soon caught on, and other chapters of The Monday Club were formed.

Other potential sources of support include:

- **Entrepreneur networks, where you will meet other entrepreneurs on a regular basis**
- **Trade associations – attend chapter meetings and meet others in the same field as you.**
- **Chambers of Commerce.**
- **Internet discussion boards or chat groups of fellow entrepreneurs.**

In this chapter, we looked at loneliness. Once you are sure that you understand that loneliness is kind of inevitable, it's time to move on to the next chapter.

QUESTION 6:
Am I the right age to start my own business?

Yes.

No, this wasn't a printing error.

The short one-word answer to the question posed in this chapter is absolutely correct. You are always the right age to start your own business.

Maybe I should expand on this a little.

What do you think is the lower age limit for starting your own business? Is it 30? 25? 20? And what do you think is the upper age limit for starting a new business? Is it 60? 70? 80?

> *We don't stop playing because we grow old; We grow old because we stop playing!*
> Nana (age 103)

If we look for inspiration to Silicon Valley, it would be easy to equate entrepreneurship with youth. Think of Jobs, Dell, Gates, Yang and others who founded industry-changing companies while still in their twenties.

CASE STUDY

Harold S. Blue, chairman of Proxymed Inc., a health-care information services company in Ft. Lauderdale, Florida, was only 10 years old when he started his first business, a neighbourhood snow removal service.

At 16, he set up a drugstore in the lobby of a new, unrented doctors building, which soon brought in renters for the owner and led to a booming business for himself.

In his 20s, Blue started a chain of discount drug stores, a generic drug distribution company, and a number of other health-care businesses.

CASE STUDY

In the winter of 1873, school dropout Chester Greenwood was trying out his new ice skates on Abbot Pond, Farmington, Maine. His ears got very cold from the icy wind. Wrapping his head in a woollen scarf proved too bulky and itchy. Because he was a farm boy, he knew all about wire, so he fashioned two ear-shaped loops, and asked his grandmother to sew fur on them. The result - the world's first earmuffs. On March 13, 1877, the United States Patent Office awarded him patent #188,292 for an improved model with a steel band that held the muffs in place. By the time he was 18, Chester had established Greenwood's Ear Protector Factory, and he went on to make a fortune supplying Ear Protectors to US soldiers during World War I. By 1936, annual output had reached 400,000 earmuffs.

CASE STUDY

When 10-year-old Kathryn Gregory from Massachusetts was playing in her yard following a harsh New England snowstorm, snow kept finding its way up the sleeve of her coat. At her mother's suggestion, she sewed some synthetic fleece into cylinders, and designed detachable sleeves that extend only as far as the palm of the hand. Then she cut a slit for the thumb, to anchor the sleeves in place. After conducting field tests, Kathryn tried out her invention on her Girl Scout troop. Encouraged by their response, she consulted a patent attorney, who confirmed that her idea was original. Kathryn herself invented the name "Wristies," and she went on to found Wristies, Inc. Within three years, Kathryn became the youngest person ever to promote a product on the QVC shopping channel. Her 6-minute spot earned her $22,000 in sales.

But industries can also be founded at the other end of the age spectrum.

CASE STUDY

When Mike Lloyd lost his job as a business advisor with a regional development organisation, he did not at first think of starting his own business. However, finding a permanent job was harder than he anticipated, possibly because he was already in his 60s. One weekend, he was visiting a garden centre where he saw an ad from a new florist wanting a driver. He decided to take the job until something else came along.

His first job was a delivery to a local undertaker. When he arrived, three separate florists' vans were also delivering flowers. Quickly realising how inefficient that was, he suggested to the florist employing him that if he invoiced him, rather than working directly for him, he could do deliveries not just for them but for all the local florists. In this way, they could all reduce their costs. So he set up Flying Flowers Network, and his delivery service was soon working with a dozen florists in the north Somerset area.

CASE STUDY

Graham Siggs spent 40 years in the RAF before he reached retirement age at 55. He joined the civil service, but had to retire at 60. As he was not yet ready for the rocking chair and slippers, he looked for an opportunity to use his technical experience. The business he started, HuntsPAT, is a testing service for portable electrical devices. Portable Appliance Testing (PAT) is the electrical equivalent of gas safety checks, which have to be carried out on appliances once a year.

Although this is not yet a legal requirement in the UK, Graham learned that the law demands that all electrical equipment must be safe. Since he had been conducting PAT tests for over 45 years, Graham had the ideal background to specialize in this field. He is convinced that his age has been an asset in setting up his business, because he has amassed wide experience in so many fields.

> *Absolutely never say to yourself, I'm too old, if you can convey your passion for what you are doing.*
> Janet Hanson, founder, Milestone Capital Management

One thing emerges very strongly from these case studies: the idea that you can be too old or too young to start your own business, is nonsense. There is no "ideal" age to start your own business, and you can never be too old or too young.

> *Starting a business at 80 is really no different from starting one at any age.*
> Doris Drucker

QUESTION 7:
Do I know in what field I want to make my mark?

At first sight, it might seem odd that we are only asking this question at this relatively late stage in the evolutionary process of entrepreneurship. After all, when the entrepreneurial urge gets to you, shouldn't you know what line of business you want to get into?

The answer is: Not necessarily.

The urge to start your own business is an emotional urge. You have to be mentally prepared to give up the ladder world when you strike out on your own. If you are lucky, then the realisation that you want to go it alone coincides with knowing what you want to do.

But it isn't always like that. It is possible to experience a strong urge to leave the ladder world without having a specific plan.

If you don't yet know in what field you want to make your entrepreneurial mark, here are some tips:

- Think back to your childhood. What used to fascinate you? What were your hobbies? What turned the cogs in your head?
- Ask yourself what you love doing that others might find boring or undesirable.
- Ask yourself what attracts your attention.

- Ask yourself what you are passionate about.
- Ask yourself what makes you mad - the flip side of this is usually something you feel passionate about.
- Ask yourself what you would really love to do if you didn't have to worry about money.
- If your Fairy Godmother granted you one wish, what would it be? What change would you make in your life?
- In what areas of life do you really excel? What sort of things have earned you compliments in the past?
- What causes you sustained joy?
- If you had a free day with absolutely no commitments, where and what would you gravitate to? Who (if anyone) would you be doing it with, and why?
- What would you choose to put on your own headstone?
- If you could write your own obituary, what would you like it to say?

In other words, you need to conduct some brainstorming – either with yourself, or with the input of others.

It is useful to distinguish between our right brain and our left brain. Our right brain is all about feeling, emotion, imagination, fantasy, symbols and images. All thoughts and ideas start in the right brain - we look at the jumble of data, and start simplifying and identifying this data. I like to think of the right brain as personified by Albert Einstein ("Why is it I get my best ideas in the morning while I'm shaving?"), the greatest scientist of the 20th century.

Our left brain uses logic, details, facts, words, language, math and science, comprehension, order/pattern perception, and practical reality. I like to use Mr Spock of Star Trek fame to embody left brain thinking. Spock was the science officer (Starfleet service number S179-276 SP) aboard the Starship Enterprise. Played by Leonard Nemoy, his mother was a human schoolteacher while his father was a diplomat from the Planet Vulcan. Spock never smiled, because humour was not rational. His favourite phrase was: "That's not logical."

In the thinking process, no sooner does Einstein come up with right-brain ideas than Spock processes the data, makes judgments, draws conclusions, evaluates their usefulness, and usually dismisses the ideas as "impractical."

As we saw earlier, schools place a higher value on Mr Spock (left brain skills such as mathematics, logic and language) than on Einstein (using our imagination.) So when you want to brainstorm, you need to tap into your hidden reservoirs of right brain creative thinking.

Here are some brainstorming tips that will help you narrow down the choices for starting your own business:

- Keep Spock outside the room – he will eventually have to be part of the brainstorming process, but his presence too early in the process is disruptive.
- Set a specific time and place for the brainstorming - no phone calls, no breaks.
- Change perspective. Think of the scene in Dead Poets Society where Robin Williams urges his students to stand on their desks. Choose a place that you are unfamiliar with.

- Define the challenge. The better you formulate and articulate what you want to come up with, (i.e. what area will I start my business?) - the better your chance of finding creative solutions.
- Don't censor your ideas - write down every single idea as it occurs to you. Don't worry if the idea doesn't make sense. Don't ask whether the idea is feasible. Don't compare ideas, don't prioritise ideas, just keep scribbling.
- Encourage silly ideas.
- Whittle down dozens of ideas to 4-5 feasible ideas.
- You may now allow Spock into the room, to help further reduce the ideas to 3, then 2, and then to 1.
- Always ask yourself: Am I going to have fun doing this? If not – maybe you need a second round of brainstorming.

When you are looking for skills that could form the basis of a new business venture, you must be honest with yourself. Just because you have a particular skill does not mean that you should necessarily build a business around that skill. On the other hand, lacking a particular skill does not mean that you can't give it a try. Whatever you choose, look for a business or career that suits your temperament and allows you to express your own individuality.

There are lots of different kinds of self-employed entrepreneurs.

- **People who start a hi-tech business**
- **People who start a low-tech business**
- **People who start a no-tech business**
- **People in manufacturing**
- **People in services**

- One-person businesses (soloists)
- People who intend to employ staff
- People who start a business with partners
- People who buy an existing business
- Micro-enterprises
- Small businesses
- Medium businesses
- Large businesses
- Brick-and-mortar operations
- Click-and-order operations
- Bricks 'n clicks operations

Some people decide to seek professional help when they are looking for a business idea. A word of warning: Be careful about whom you listen to about career advice.

CASE STUDY

Before he left school, a student received unsolicited career advice from two of his teachers. One teacher said to him, "You're a good B. So don't set your sights too high. Don't have ideas above your abilities. You are not A material, but you're also no dunce. There's no point applying to get into top colleges like Oxford or Cambridge University. Apply to a good solid regional university." The student thanked the teacher, and duly got a B grade in every subject in his final exams. He attended a good B university, and got a B grade in his BA.

The other teacher said, "Whatever you do, don't write." The student said, "Thank you, Miss. May I ask why not?" "Because you lack imagination," she replied. The student thanked her, and for the next 15 years, he did not put creative pen to paper.

After completing two university degrees and floundering in a succession of dead-end ladder jobs, the student decided to go out on his own. He started his own marketing communication business, offering copywriting services to ad agencies and design studios. Eventually, he wrote several books and had a regular column in the newspaper.

I can personally vouch for the truthfulness of this last case study. That student was me!

As the following case studies show, people can fall into new businesses and new industries almost by mistake.

CASE STUDY

Carl Magee of Oklahoma City was already a successful newspaper editor when he was invited in 1935 to join the city's Chamber of Commerce Traffic Committee. When he attended his first meeting, he found that his committee colleagues were trying to solve the city's chronic parking congestion. There were fears that if nothing was done soon, the situation threatened to bring the traffic to a standstill.

As he listened to the deliberations, Magee started doodling on a piece of paper. He had in mind a way of disincentivising drivers from hogging all the parking spaces along the main streets. It occurred to him that the best way to make drivers aware of the problem was through their pocket. Magee sketched a crude drawing of a machine that would accept coins in exchange for parking time.

At that moment, the idea of meter parking was born. Quickly realising the potential of parking meters, Magee created the Dual Parking Meter Co. The company's first product was the

Park-O-Meter. Thus was born the global meter parking industry.

> **CASE STUDY**

Lawyer Warren Brown worked as a successful federal litigator, but he just wasn't happy in his work. One of the ways he found to release the stress of his job was to whip up cakes and throw dessert parties for his friends. The friends were highly enthusiastic about Warren's cakes, and he decided to take leave of absence from his government job to become a baker.

He subleased a small commercial kitchen, and most of his customers arrived through word of mouth. The business grew steadily, and Warren decided to make the bold move of renting a 600-square-foot storefront. He called the business Cake Love, and opened the Love Cafe across the street from his Cake Love bakery. His unusual story won him appearances on Oprah and the Today show.

A word about hopping back and forth between the employee world and the self-employed world. I have a friend who is an "on-again, off-again entrepreneur." I met him for coffee just after he left his own start-up business to return once again to the corporate world. I asked him about the job and his response was less than enthusiastic. "What's wrong?" I asked him.

"I work in a tiny office space, I have to commute long hours every day, and I have to face the boredom of a 9 to 5 work day. I only took this job because I recently got married and I needed the extra security." Suddenly, he pulled out a business card - which did not have the name of his new employer. "This is a small business that I'm starting to run part-time from home. If everything works out, I'll be back working at home and running a business from my laptop."

On-again off-again entrepreneurs are simply entrepreneurs who take corporate jobs because they need money, but at heart they want to do their own thing. For them, the question is less a matter of Should I, Shouldn't I, and more a question of Should I Now or Should I Later.

To summarise this chapter, I believe that it is preferable to have the right entrepreneurial mindset without a specific plan, than to have a plan without the right entrepreneurial mindset.

In other words, first you must really want to start your own business. Next, you have to choose in what area you want to start a business. Then you have to give it full throttle.

QUESTION 8:
Should I work from home?

In Question 5, we identified choice as the most important benefit of working for yourself. Some people choose to work alone. They do not want partners or staff. Such go-it-alone people are described variously as:

- **Soloists**
- **Freelancers**
- **Solo operators**
- **Sole traders**
- **Sole proprietors**
- **Consultants**
- **Contractors**
- **Lone wolves**

If you choose to be a soloist, you may not necessarily be interested in pioneering new technologies. You may be more interested in building a career than equity, and you don't always dream of empire building. But you can be driven by the same sense of excitement, enthusiasm, energy and motivation as entrepreneurs who go on to create much larger businesses.

One of the choices available to the new business owner is the choice to run your business from your own home. More and more people are now exercising this option, either as a short-term solution, while they search for suitable premises, or as a permanent solution, as an alternative to working from a dedicated workplace.

Before you decide to turn your home into a home-based business, you need to establish whether your business lends itself to being operated out of your home.

Here is a partial list of businesses that can be run from your home.

- Accountant
- Alternative medical practitioner
- Architect
- Artist
- Beautician
- Business consultant
- Children's party organiser
- Clown
- Computer repair
- Copywriter
- Desk Top Publishing
- Event management
- Export/Import
- Freelance secretarial services
- Graphic designer
- Hairdresser
- Health and fitness professional
- House painter
- Interior designer
- Marriage counsellor
- Marketing consultant
- Masseur/masseuse
- Nutritionist
- Party organiser
- Pet sitting and boarding
- Photographer
- Physician
- Physiotherapist
- Plasterer
- Plumber
- PR consultant
- Programmer
- Property consultant
- Signwriter
- Small manufacturer
- Software designer
- Substance abuse counsellor
- Surveyor
- Telemarketing
- Trainer
- Web designer
- Wedding car hire
- Writer

People who choose to work from home do so for a host of different reasons:

- **No more rush-hour commute**
- **No boss breathing down your neck**
- **No fixed schedule**
- **More reward for your effort**
- **Greater control**
- **Work/family flexibility**
- **Not having to worry about being laid off**
- **Leaving the office politics behind you**
- **Not having to get dressed up**
- **Spending more time with children/family**
- **Cost savings**
- **Working fewer hours**

If you decide to work from home, you will not usually make use of every single room. Based on your needs, you will allocate some specif c part of your home to serve as your office. Here are some of spaces in your home that can be converted to home business use:

- **Basement**
- **Attic**
- **Garage**
- **Under the staircase**
- **Garden shed**
- **Mobile home in the garden**
- **Living room**
- **Kitchen table**
- **Converted bedroom**

The business media has variously described stay-at-home self-employed entrepreneurs as mumpreneurs, dadpreneurs, and the pyjama set (based on the assumption that people who work from home hang around all day in their pyjamas.)

Running a business from home is more than just finding a suitable business and a physical working space. It is also about whether you are temperamentally suited to run your business out of your home.

Any new business involves the need to find a dynamic equilibrium between the demands of the business and the demands of family life. When you work from home, finding this equilibrium is even more critical.

Here are 20 questions you need to ask yourself if you're thinking of working from home:

1. Do I have the self-discipline to work from home?
2. Will I be able to motivate myself to sit down and work on whatever needs to be done?
3. Can I withstand the distractions?
4. Can I successfully separate my home life from my work life?
5. Can I successfully separate my home space from my work space?
6. Can I lay down rules for how I will use my home office?
7. Can I turn my home office into a private sanctuary?
8. Am I prepared to hang a "Do Not Disturb" sign on the door of my home office?
9. Can I set clearly defined boundaries for the other members of the family?
10. Will the members of my family respect my rules?

11. How will I cope with unexpected interruptions (doorbell, neighbour, kids, dog)?
12. How will my family react if I want to have staff working in my home?
13. Will I succeed in staying away from household tasks during the time I have allocated for work?
14. Do I need a fire inspection permit or a sign permit?
15. Where will I meet with clients who come to my home?
16. Will visitors be able to reach my office/work space without walking through my home?
17. Do I want to set a limit to my after-hours work?
18. Do I need liability coverage in the event that a client is injured on my property?
19. Am I sure that the local zoning laws allow me to run a business from home?
20. If I expect my family to pitch in and help me, have I discussed this with them?

> *The free-lance writer is a man who is paid per piece or per word or perhaps.*
> Robert Benchley

When you work from home and you have a family, they become involved in your business, even if they have no official role. There is always a danger that family members can get the mistaken impression that because you're at home, you are available for errands. You may need to educate your family – partner, kids, parents, pets - that when you are working in your business space, you are off-limits.

In an earlier chapter, we saw how lonely it can be when you start your own business. This can be compounded further when you work from home.

- You may miss the contact with your work colleagues.
- You may miss the buzz of a hectic office environment.
- You may develop cabin fever.

Here are some hints that will help you break the monotony and work more effectively and efficiently from home:

- Create a dedicated physically separate space, as far as possible from the living space. Use furniture that suits the dimensions of your space, rather than trying to work around standard size office furniture.
- Make sure you can close the door to your work space.
- Make sure that your workspace has easily accessible electrical outlets, and that the lighting and ventilation are appropriate to your kind of work.
- Organise a ruthlessly efficient filing system that takes up minimum space.
- Inform your family members if you are under particular pressure, and avoid making personal calls while you are in your work space.
- Dress in a way that helps you work productively.
- Schedule appointments in a neutral venue (hotel lobby, coffee shop) rather than in your home. If you must meet clients at home, your office must look like a "real" business where you can negotiate across a desk or table in a business-like atmosphere.
- Get out and take a break from the routine. Do some stretching exercises, take a walk around the block.
- Create a more professional image for your home business by adding "Suite 1102" to your address, to give the impression that your business is in an office complex.

QUESTION 9:
Do I have what it takes to be my own boss?

A question I am frequently asked is: "What entrepreneurial qualities and entrepreneurial prerequisites do I need if I want to start my own business?"

Business guru Jim Rohn lists 10 qualities that entrepreneurs need that are more valuable than start-up capital:

1. Ambition
2. Time
3. Desperation
4. Determination.
5. Courage
6. Faith.
7. Ingenuity
8. Heart and Soul.
9. Personality
10. Charisma

American psychologist John D Gartner suggests 10 entrepreneurial attributes:

1. Grand ambitions
2. Energy
3. Ideas
4. Restlessness
5. Euphoria
6. Risk-taking

7. Impulsiveness
8. Fast-talking
9. Wittiness
10. Irritation at obstacles

The Entrepreneurship Forum of New England identified 6 qualities that make an entrepreneur:

1. Dreamer
2. Innovator
3. Passionate
4. Risk taker
5. Dogged Committer
6. Continuous Learner

Ryan P. M. Allis, author of *From Zero to One Million*, asked successful entrepreneurs to rank 15 entrepreneurial qualities. This is how they prioritised the list:

1. Being able to build a solid team
2. Leadership and the ability to inspire
3. Persistence
4. Motivation and ambition
5. Integrity
6. Ability to communicate effectively
7. Confidence
8. Being able to execute
9. Having a bias toward action
10. Having a good idea or plan
11. Knowledge of marketing
12. Good networking skills
13. Having the right advisors
14. Knowledge of accounting and finance
15. A college degree

(I find it fascinating that knowledge of accounting and having a college degree came last!)

The Marriott Center for Entrepreneurship identifies no less than 33 entrepreneurial qualities:

1. Confident
2. Risk taker
3. Hard working
4. Creative
5. Flexible
6. Busy, time consuming, long hours
7. Dedication
8. Effort
9. Believer
10. Enjoys what he/she does
11. Driven, has a reason
12. Great sacrifices
13. Passion/love for what they do
14. Committed
15. Never quits
16. Doesn't know how to relax
17. Impersonal, task oriented
18. Doesn't stay within the lines the company sets
19. Unorganized
20. C or D student, has their own ideas
21. Visionary
22. Courageous
23. Headstrong/stubborn
24. Idealistic
25. Self-motivated
26. Innovative
27. Problem solvers
28. Won't take no for an answer

29. Stressful
30. Able to overcome challenges/negatives
31. Jack of all trades, good at a lot of things
32. Perfectionist
33. Knows where he/she is going and where he/she wants to be.

Just as every cake must have a good mix of the right ingredients, your personal entrepreneurial cake needs the right mix of entrepreneurial ingredients.

Here is my list of entrepreneurial qualities:

1   Self-confidence and self-belief

It is difficult to imagine how anyone can start a business without a healthy quotient of self-confidence, self-esteem and self-belief. If your business venture is going to succeed, you must believe in yourself. If you agonise over every decision, and constantly worry about whether you did the right thing, you may never get your business off the ground.

> *If people believe in themselves, it's amazing what they can accomplish.*
> Sam Walton

Some of the hallmarks of self-confidence:

- I have a great belief in myself
- I believe that nothing is impossible
- I know I can master whatever it takes to start my own business
- I know that I am capable of accomplishing anything I set my mind to.

- I like to rely on myself
- I have the self-confidence to follow my own vision
- I don't understand why I shouldn't do something just because it hasn't been done before.
- I know that my way is the best way
- I prefer to do something myself rather than rely on others.
- I don't waste time wondering whether I did the right thing
- I am not plagued by doubt
- I am comfortable with self-promotion

SELF-CONFIDENT PEOPLE	PEOPLE WHO LACK SELF-CONFIDENCE
Take risks and go the extra mile to achieve extraordinary things.	Remain in their comfort zone, fear failure and avoid taking risks.
Admit their mistakes and learn from them.	Work hard to cover up mistakes and hope that nobody notices them.
Do not seek - yet graciously accept - compliments on their accomplishments.	Extol their own virtues as often as possible to as many people as possible.
View challenges as opportunities to learn and grow.	Feel desperate when things don't go exactly as planned.
Put a positive spin on negative things that happen.	Dwell on negative events and often use them as reasons to quit.

Remember: being confident is not the same as being extrovert or talking loudly. Although I freely admit that I am an extrovert and I that my decibel level is high, I know plenty of people who express their confidence in a much quieter manner. And that's fine.

> *When you have confidence, you can have a lot of fun. And when you have fun, you can do amazing things,*
> Joe Namath

2   Being proactive

There is no room for shyness when you own your own business. Your primary responsibility as a business owner is to find the most effective ways of bringing your business to the notice of your potential clients. And that means being upfront and upbeat about your business, your products and your services.

Starting your own business requires a proactive state of mind. You can't sit and wait for things to happen – because they won't. "If it's to be, it's up to me," is the motto in the entrepreneurial world. Nothing happens unless you make it happen. Initiative is a daily, even an hourly, matter. There are all sorts of things that require action. Many unsuccessful business people procrastinate about taking action on critical matters.

> *Inaction breeds doubt and fear. Action breeds confidence and courage. If you want to conquer fear, do not sit home and think about it. Go out and get busy.*
> Dale Carnegie

Entrepreneurs are doers. They are quick to take the initiative. They are driven. They are quick to spot and seize opportunities. They are proactive. They want to get on with things. They relish challenges. They don't sit around waiting for things to happen, they rush out to meet them. They need to feel in control of the situation.

CASE STUDY

There was a certain inevitability that Bud Hatfield would end up in the printing business. In junior high school he ran a print shop in his basement called The Family News. As a youngster, he went around his neighbourhood in Cranston, Rhode Island, selling door to door ad sales, business cards and stationery print work. But although Hatfield developed a reputation as an enterprising young man with a lot of initiative, this did not immediately translate into business success. After a string of business failures, he headed for Houston in 1948 where he opened a small letterpress printing shop. In 1967 he opened Kwik Kopy, and his whole world changed. The man who had shown such initiative as a youngster went on to become head of the world's largest international alliances of printing and copying franchises.

> *Don't just stand there, make it happen.*
> Lee Iacocca

3   Single-Mindedness and Focus

If there is one thing about the entrepreneurial experience that is guaranteed, t is that there will plenty of surprises and obstacles along the way. Goal posts will move, people will let you down, and unexpected scenarios will disturb your plans.

You need to be very focussed. You can't afford to be sidetracked. You are not doing this for the short haul, so you always need to keep the bigger picture in mind. If you believe in something, keep at it.

> *The secret of success is constancy of purpose.*
> Benjamin Disraeli

This is why you need to be able to persist with your ideas, and to single-mindedly persist with your hard work. We use many different words to describe the kind of single-mindedness you need as an entrepreneur.

- **Determination**
- **Focus**
- **Persistence**
- **Steadfastness**
- **Stubbornness**
- **Perseverance**
- **Tenacity**
- **Pig-headedness**
- **Willpower**
- **Resolve**
- **Doggedness**
- **Endurance**
- **Resoluteness**
- **Decisiveness**
- **Discipline**

CASE STUDY

Kentucky high school student Patricia Galloway was a dancer, a member of the drama club, a keen debater and an artist. One day, she attended an obligatory lecture by a professor from the University of Kentucky. He was a structural civil engineer, and he had brought along to the class several renderings of buildings. When the professor said that women had great opportunities in the engineering field, Pat was hooked. There and then, she decided to become a civil engineer. Her teachers were less than enthusiastic. Her career guidance counsellor said, "Bad idea. You have not scored on your aptitude test to be an engineer. You're not inclined to be an engineer. You're not made up to be an engineer." Her grandmother said, "Isn't that a man's job?" And even when she was accepted to Purdue University's school of engineering, one professor told her, "You should not be here because women should not be in engineering."

Pat was determined to prove them all wrong. She graduated in 1978 with a B+ degree in civil engineering, went on to earn an MBA in Finance from New York Institute of Technology's Executive MBA program, and became a professional engineer (PE) and Project Management Professional (PMP). She became CEO and Principal of the Nielsen-Wurster Group, an international management consulting and dispute resolution company, and she became the first ever woman to serve as president of the American Society of Civil Engineers.

4   Inquisitiveness, imagination and visualisation

> *Imagination is more important than knowledge.*
> Albert Einstein

You probably would never have thought of starting your own business unless you were inquisitive. You have to keep an eye out for anything that could affect your business. You must keep up to date with new ideas, new methods and new trends. You must be aware of the wider business context within which you operate, and you have to know what the competition is doing and planning. You must always be looking out for innovative ways of doing things.

If you can imagine and visualise your business and how it will run, you will find it much easier to fill in the dots. Visualisation helps to bring your entrepreneurial dream to life. If you can get excited about what you visualise, this excitement will spur you on to turn it into reality.

Peter Drucker claims that the three makers of the modern world were Darwin, Freud and Taylor. Everyone knows who Freud and Darwin were. But who was Taylor?

CASE STUDY

Frederick Winslow Taylor was born in 1856. He gave up a chance to study at Harvard, and instead signed on for four years as an apprentice at a small Philadelphia pump works. He worked his way up from labourer in the machine shop to chief engineer. And during this whole period, Taylor never stopped watching everyone and everything. His inquisitiveness led him to try and understand the nature of work. He started breaking down work tasks into constituent elements, timing each element based on repeated stopwatch studies, and fixing compensation based on those studies.

It was Taylor who introduced the concept of scientific management. Taylor thought that by scientifically analysing work, he could find the "One Best Way" to do it. He is most remembered for developing the time and motion study that broke jobs into their component parts and measure each to the second. One of his most famous studies involved shovels. He noticed that the workers used the same shovel for all materials. After determining that the most effective load was 21 lb, he designed different shovels to scoop up the exact amount for each material. Efficiency rocketed as a result.

And even though some of Taylor's ideas proved to be a little too much for some people to stomach, his incessant inquisitiveness led to insights that help us in the workplace to this day.

5   Accepting a certain level of risk, uncertainty and ambiguity

> *The only thing that makes life possible is permanent, intolerable uncertainty.*
> Ursula K. LeGuin

Every new business venture contains an element of risk. But that doesn't mean that you need to thrive on risk in order to start your own business. It's a question of definition. From the outside looking in, entrepreneurs are characterised as risk takers. From the inside looking out, it feels like something that you simply have to do if you want to follow your own star.

> *If you don't risk anything you risk even more.*
> Erica Jong

Compared to the so-called security of working for someone else, starting your own business can look risky. Yet in this era of increasing globalisation, thousands of jobs can be lost in an instant. All it takes is for your employer to discover an alternative, cheaper source of labour somewhere else in the world, and you could be history. With market pressures now dictating the employment market, and the old ties of loyalty fading into distant memory, there is almost as much risk associated with staying employed as starting your own business.

> *First weigh the considerations, then take the risks.*
> Helmuth von Moltke

Business never goes in predictable directions, and you must be able to survive in an unstructured environment. When you start your own business, you need to be able cope with uncertainty and ambiguity. Structure and certainty are seldom found in the entrepreneurial world.

You must learn to thrive in an environment that is confusing and has few answers. There is never a guarantee that the products or services that you offer now will still be in demand in six months time. Uncertainty surrounds when and even whether your customers will pay you, and there is always the danger that your current major client may drop you next week. You have to learn to think on your feet, remain flexible, and not to be thrown by every change of plan.

> *And the day came when the risk to remain tight in a bud was more painful than the risk it took to blossom.*
> Anais Nin

6 Not being devastated by adversity, discouragement or begrudgery

It's sad but true: not everyone is on your side when you start your own business. There will be those who doubt your business vision. There will be funders who laugh at your application for a start-up loan. There will be potential customers who don't appreciate your brilliance. And there will be short-sighted suppliers who don't believe you are credit-worthy.

If the Wright Brothers had listened to the words of celebrated inventor Lord Kelvin: "I have not the smallest molecule of faith in aerial navigation" – they might never have gone on to perform the first-ever powered air flight.

If schoolboy G K Chesterton had listened to what his teacher wrote in his report: "If we could open your head, we should not find any brain but only a lump of white fat," he may never have written over 100 books.

If Richard Rodgers and Oscar Hammerstein had listened to the comments of impresario Mike Todd, who described their new musical as: "No legs, no jokes, no chance," *Oklahoma* would never have become one of the most successful musicals in history. If Norma Jean Baker had followed the advice of the Blue Book modelling agency, she would have become a secretary instead of becoming Marilyn Monroe.

When Anthony Sher was a young unknown actor freshly arrived in London from South Africa, he auditioned for Rada, the Royal Academy of Dramatic Arts. The letter informing him that he had failed to get a place in this prestigious drama school said: "Not only have you failed, and you must not try again, but we most seriously urge you to think of a different career." Sher turned out to be one of the most gifted actors of his generation. If he had listened to this disastrous advice, we would have been robbed of an amazing talent.

"Cat in the Hat" author Theodor Geiselk, also known as Dr Seuss, who became one of the most prolific and famous children's authors of all time, had his first book rejected by 23 publishers. Thomas Edison tried to dissuade Henry Ford from producing his Model T Ford car (the one that you could buy in any colour so long as it was black.)

Albert Einstein's father was told by his high school teacher: "It doesn't matter what he does – he will never amount to anything." Einstein was later refused a place at the Munich Technical Institute because he "showed no promise."

When Stephen R. Covey broke the news to his father that instead of joining the family hotel and property empire, he intended to become a leadership trainer, his father repeated the old adage: "Those who can, do. Those who can't, teach." This negative response did not deter Covey, who went on to write the best selling *The 7 Habits of Successful People*.

> *The most essential factor is the determination never to allow your energy or enthusiasm to be dampened by the discouragement that must inevitably come.*
> James Whitcomb Riley

CASE STUDY

John Warnock is an engineer who helped found Adobe Systems Inc., the company that helped launch the desktop publishing revolution. After flunking algebra at school, he was told to take an aptitude test. At the interview after the test, he was told: "You should probably consider not going to college. What do you think you'd like to do?" At that time, John had no clear idea of his future plans, so he said, "Well, maybe something like engineering." To which the counsellor replied: "Your probability of having any kind of success in any engineering-related activity is probably zero."

When you encounter negativity, remember that envy, jealousy, spite and begrudgery are all about other people's agendas.

There is no point trying to please everyone, even those close to you. Lift your head above the negativity, and do what you have to do.

CASE STUDY

After working as a cook in a vegetarian restaurant, and as a research assistant in an economic consultancy, Antonia Rolls took a career break to raise a family. Adversity struck when just after the birth of her third child, Antonia's husband left her, taking all their money with him. Antonia was very overweight, she had three small kids to raise alone, and she was at a very low ebb.

Yet it precisely at this point that Antonia returned to her passion for painting. With nothing to lose, she decided to become what she had always secretly believed she could become - a successful artist. Within three years, she had found a studio, networked with other artists, and started selling her paintings. She also lost nearly 30 kilo, started participating in studio exhibitions, and began to define herself as an artist. Such was her growing confidence that she came up with the title 'Artist Extraordinaire'.

> **Keep away from people who try to belittle your ambitions. Small people always do that.**
> Mark Twain

7   Refusing to accept the failure label

Failure is not an objective yardstick, so we shouldn't accept anyone else's definition. We only fail when we give up trying. The real test is how we handle failure and what we can learn from it.

Just because you close your business does not mean that it has failed. Wrigley's began life as a soap manufacturer. When they used chewing gum as a promotion for their soap powder, they realised that they could make much more money selling chewing gum, so they eventually closed down their soap business. Was Wrigley's a failure?

CASE STUDY

He drifted from job to job, and eventually opened a dry goods shop in Boston. When this did not succeed, he joined the California Gold Rush, and opened another dry goods store. The business folded, and was sold at public auction. He returned to his native Massachusetts and opened yet another dry goods store. When this failed, he tried his luck in Superior City, a boom-town in Wisconsin. This venture also failed, so he moved into real estate. The boom-town stopped booming, and again he lost money. He moved to New York City, where he opened a small fancy goods store. He could not afford premises in the main shopping district, so he settled for a store-front in a location where several other businesses had failed. Within two months, the store was robbed and there was a fire. But he did not give up. He gradually added new lines of merchandise, and eventually bought the surrounding stores. Despite a dozen years of consistent business failures, he refused to accept the failure label. His name? Rowland Hussey Macy, founder of Macy's Department Store.

Many of the most famous entrepreneurs in history had a string of failures before they finally made it. Walt Disney made a loss on his first five business ventures. Donald Trump made millions, lost millions, and made them all back again.

Not being devastated by failure also means not beating yourself up for absolutely everything that happens. Some things really are out of your control. If you take the blame for everything, you'll be carrying the weight of the world on your shoulders. Instead of forever saying to yourself: "Why did I do that?" "Why am I such an idiot? – decide to learn a valuable lesson. There's no more powerful learning than the learning that comes from your own mistakes.

CASE STUDY

He tried his hand at business and he failed. He ran for the political office of State Legislature, and he lost. He went back to another business venture. Again he failed. He tried politics again. He wanted to make a difference. He ran for office once again, and was elected to the State Legislature. But when he ran for Speaker of the House, he lost. He ran for Congress. He was elected, but when he ran for a second term, he lost.

A few years later, he ran for the U.S. Senate. He failed to get elected. He ran for Vice President of the United States, and lost again. Two years later he tried again for U.S. Senate, and failed once more. Two years later, he ran for the Presidency, and became the sixteenth President of the United States. He also became one of the most famous and influential people in world history. The name of the man who refused to accept the label "loser," who ignored failure, and who hung on to his dream: Abraham Lincoln.

> *When I was a young man, I observed that nine out of ten things I did were failures. I didn't want to be a failure, so I did ten times more work.*
> George Bernard Shaw

Failure is always a relative term. It so depends on whether you are on the inside looking out, or on the outside looking in.

8   Energy

They say that unless you are prepared to work hard, you should not start a company. I actually think it's the other way round. Unless you already work hard, you should not start a company – because it is unlikely that you can easily pick up this crucial habit. Atari founder Nolan Bushnell said that it all comes down to one critical ingredient: "Getting off your ass and doing something."

A high energy level is a must if you are starting your own business. You will need to be prepared to put in a constant and consistent effort, and devote long hours to your business. When those hours will be of course depends on the kind of business. A morning person might not do well running a business that requires staying up late, while a night person might not be very happy running an early morning delivery business.

You need to give your business 100 percent. Your customers need to know that you are devoting 100 percent of your time and focus to their needs.

QUESTION 10:
Do I have the passion, the fire in the belly and the chutzpah?

In Question #9, we looked at some core entrepreneurial qualities you need. In this chapter, we identify some extra qualities.

One is passion. You have to be passionate about your new business. You must feel a burning desire to nurture your business, commit to it, and passionately work for its success.

> *You're only given a little spark of madness. You mustn't lose it.*
> Robin Williams

You also need to passionately protect your business. It's the same sort of pride you have for your family, your home, your car or when a new baby is born. You created your business, and you are responsible for its success.

THE MOUNTAIN

There were two tribes in the Andes. One tribe lived in a village in the lowlands, at the foot of the mountain, and the other tribe lived in a village high in the mountains. One day, a raiding party of mountain people invaded the lowlanders. They kidnapped a lowlander baby and took the infant with them back up into the mountains.

The lowlanders didn't know how to climb the mountain. They didn't know any of the trails that the mountain people used. They didn't know where to find the mountain people or how to track them in the steep terrain.

Nevertheless, the lowlanders sent out a party of their strongest men to climb the mountain and bring the baby home. The men tried one method of climbing and then another. They tried one trail and then another. But after several days of effort, they had only climbed a few hundred feet.

Feeling hopeless, the lowlanders decided that there was no point continuing, and they prepared to return to their village below.

As they were packing their gear for the descent, they saw a figure emerging from the mist. Then they saw that it was the baby's mother walking towards them.

She was coming down the mountain - and here they were, unable to figure out how to climb up any further.

The lowlanders then noticed that she had the baby strapped to her back. In amazement, they asked her: "How were you able to climb this mountain when we, the strongest and most able men in the village, could not?"

She shrugged her shoulders and said:

"It wasn't your baby."

If you have passion and enthusiasm, you have fire in the belly - the culmination of all the other entrepreneurial qualities and prerequisites.

Fire in the Belly is also the name of my first book: *Fire in the Belly – an exploration of the entrepreneurial spirit.*

> *Knowledge is power and enthusiasm pulls the switch.*
> Steve Droke

I have often been asked, why fire in the belly? Why not fire in the brain, or fire in the heart?

The answer of course is that the belly is the seat of our emotions. That's where our guts are. That's where we feel the butterflies in our stomach. The decision to start your own business is not merely a rational decision fuelled by logic, strategy or money. The decision is an emotional one.

> *We may affirm absolutely that nothing great in the world has been accomplished without passion.*
> Hegel

With fire in the belly, you have the right tools to embark on your entrepreneurial odyssey. With fire in the belly, you feel invincible. Best of all, all the fire trucks in the world cannot extinguish the fire in your belly.

You will need bucket-loads of passion and fire in the belly to help you nurture your new business.

> *If people never did silly things, nothing intelligent would ever happen.*
> Ludwig Wittgenstein

You also need to be a little crazy to leave the safe haven of the corporate world and open your own business. It's axiomatic. You have to be off-the-wall to want to go it alone in the face of the frightening statistics that inform you that for every 100 entrepreneurs who opened their new business yesterday, over half will have gone out of business within the next three years.

> ***If at first an idea is not absurd, it has no hope.***
> Albert Einstein

When you embark on the entrepreneurial journey, it should feel like fun. You are allowed to enjoy yourself. You are allowed to give your impish sense of humour an opportunity to express itself. This won't take away from the importance of your venture, and will allow you to enjoy the journey even more.

CASE STUDY

When toymaker Mattel, famous for the Barbie dolls, was looking for ways of growing beyond Barbie, they asked Ivy Ross, senior VP of worldwide design and packaging for the girls division, to come up with a new toy for girls. Ivy knew that sewing kits and jewellery kits were hot with girls, but she did not want Mattel to enter this field with a me-too product. She also knew that Lego-like construction sets had traditionally been seen as a boy's thing.

And then the fun idea struck her – why not come up with a construction toy for girls? She knew that she had to come up with something really innovative, something that was part construction set, part craft kit. Ivy had previously worked as a product designer, and was always inspired by her father, a Studebaker designer, who taught her that if you're trying to design a new car, you don't just look at other cars.

So Ivy assembled an ad hoc team of industrial designers, graphic designers, model makers, advertising copywriters and project leaders, and basically locked them away for 12 weeks.

She brought in a group of girls, and the team studied the way the girls played with pipe cleaners, cardboard, and other basic items. The girls constructed rooms and houses, they made jewellery and characters, and they told stories about the world that they had created.

Within the 12 weeks that Ivy had allocated to the task, the project team unveiled the Ello creation system for girls aged 5-10. With Ello, girls could create anything they could imagine, funky characters, room accessories, jewellery, houses and much more. The colourful pieces were easy to snap together, allowing girls to build, change and rearrange to their hearts' content.

This sense of fun is closely connected with another quality that is very helpful for entrepreneurs: Chutzpah. This evocative term, which originates in ancient Aramaic but is now common currency in the USA and increasingly in English-speaking Europe, is a combination of nerve, verve, cheek, balls, daring and audacity.

> *I firmly believe in chutzpah - that terrific Yiddish word for gall, guts, the drive to put yourself ahead.*
> Helen Gurley Brown

Chutzpah is best understood in context. Here are some people who leveraged their chutzpah to achieve their goals.

CASE STUDY

Cora Barnes, Cathie O'Reilly and Gerry Lynch started their own recruitment company, Three Q, after they were not happy with the business practices of the recruitment company they worked for. They named their company Three Q because they wanted to provide quality service using qualified staff in the quantity that clients required.

When the company was still in its infancy, the partners were chasing a contract from Dublin's prestigious Shelbourne Hotel. After months of badgering and persuasion, the hotel suddenly called Three Q just before the weekend. "We need two waitresses to do the breakfast shift tomorrow morning." It was too late to find anyone to do the work, so Cathie and Cora had to resort to chutzpah.

They got up in the middle of the night, and reported for duty at the hotel at 6am, claiming to the manager who had called the agency that they wanted to ensure that the site was looked after properly. The manager realised what had happened, but was so impressed with their chutzpah that she became a major client of Three Q.

> **The really successful people I know all have Chutzpah and are proud of it. I believe my personal success comes from having the guts, the nerve, and the no fear attitude which allows me to live fully, freely and without fear.**
> Terri Levine, CEO, Comprehensive Coaching U, Inc.

In her review of Erica Jong's memoir, *Seducing the Demon: Writing for My Life,* Elissa Strauss wrote that instead of giving her readers tips on writing, Jong was offering them tips on chutzpah — an endeavour that itself takes a little chutzpah. According to Strauss, that is precisely the nature of chutzpah. It takes chutzpah to come up with chutzpah strategies.

CASE STUDY

A few weeks before he was due to enrol as a mature student to study business management in Nottingham University, Alex Tew wondered whether he had made the right decision to study full-time after three years of hopping from one lousy job to another. He was broke, and the prospect of running up over £20,000 debt in fees over the next three years did not appeal to him. He decided to brainstorm around the question: How can I raise the funds I need? The attributes that he wrote down were: the idea had to be simple to understand and to set up; it had to attract a lot of media interest; and it needed a good name.

He came up with the idea of creating a website called the Million Dollar Homepage on which he would sell exactly one million pixels (the tiny dots that make up an image on a screen) at $1 per pixel. Alex divided his website into 10,000 boxes, each containing 100 pixels, and offered advertisers the opportunity of buying one or more boxes for $100 each. Each box or set of boxes is covered by the advertiser's logo, which, when clicked on, transports web users to the customers' own site.

Once he had sold the first 10 boxes to family and friends, Alex used the $1,000 to pay for a press release that was picked up by the BBC. News of his exploits went viral across the Internet, and within days, Alex's web address began appearing on chat rooms, and dozens of firms had signed up. The actor Jack Black, star of School of Rock and Shallow Hal, is using the site to advertise his band Tenacious D. All the indications are that Alex will sell all 1 million pixels – not bad for a student looking to cover his £20,000 tuition fees.

Chutzpah is the secret weapon in your armoury as you create, promote and grow your own business. Chutzpah means taking a leap of faith when the odds are against you.

> *A little chutzpah is a vital element in every entrepreneur's toolkit.*
> Ed Zimmer

I believe that every entrepreneur has a spark of chutzpah. It's in our DNA. When you use chutzpah, you are reverting to the daring and cheeky child you once were. You need to reclaim your chutzpah. You need to kick-start the chutzpah mindset. You need to stretch your imagination, and open the door for chutzpah to walk in.

Ask yourself:

"What would happen if….?"
"Wouldn't it be fun if….?"
"Wouldn't it be wild if….?"

Tell yourself:

"If I had the balls, I would….."
"If I dared, I would…"
"If I had the nerve, I would…."

Imagination is the mechanism that triggers a chutzpah action. You have the potential to come up with chutzpah solutions, to experience chutzpah moments, and to be blessed with flashes of chutzpah.

In *Chutzpah – unlocking the maverick mindset for success*, I offer a variety of ways in which we can use our chutzpah to our advantage:

- Chutzpah means having the nerve to go for what you want.
- Chutzpah means having the guts to leave your comfort zone.
- Chutzpah means walking boldly where others fear to tread.
- Chutzpah means thinking way outside of the box.
- Chutzpah means allowing your imagination to run riot.
- Chutzpah means a readiness to bend the rules.
- Chutzpah is seeing the extraordinary in the ordinary.
- Chutzpah is stretching the boundaries of creative imagination.
- Chutzpah is standing out from the crowd.
- Chutzpah means defying conventional wisdom and conventional logic.
- Chutzpah means zigzagging around locked doors.
- Chutzpah means thinking innovatively and laterally.
- Chutzpah means being prepared to fundamentally rethink the things around you.

Your chutzpah is waiting for you to exploit it in the service of your enterprise!

Should I, Shouldn't I?

The decision whether or not to embark on the entrepreneurial journey – the Should I, Shouldn't I? dilemma - is an intensely personal mater.

We are all taught that getting a job is the safest and most secure way to make a living.

But for many people, this can often turn out to be a myth. Employment is not necessarily either safe or secure.

In today's changing job world, being an employee – rather than being self-employed - could even be the riskier option.

If things go wrong, the entrepreneur can often be in better shape to regroup and try something else, compared to the employee who is reeling from the shock and trauma of being fired.

We started this book by focusing on why it is that we all start our working lives as employees.

We need to understand this if we are to usefully explore the transition you need to make when you move into the self-employed camp.

And we saw that the best way to discover whether you are mentally fit to make this transition is via 10 key questions.

1   You asked yourself whether you dared to leave the security of the employment world.

Can you contemplate being permanently off the employment ladder, being solely responsible for your own fate? This is not a simple question. The idea of entrepreneurship might seem attractive, but for most people, it is nevertheless an emotional wrench. You have to be sure that you are ready for it.

2   You asked yourself whether you trust the reason that triggered your decision to go out on your own.

There are lots of different triggers that can catapult you off the employment ladder and propel you towards self-employment. How reliable is your trigger? Are you being pushed to start a new business, or are you being pulled by a compelling opportunity? Have you considered the alternative of looking for another job if you are not happy with your present job?

3   You asked yourself whether you could cope with a less than enthusiastic response from your family.

Never underestimate the power of your family to dampen your enthusiasm for your new business. They don't do this because they hate you. On the contrary, they tell you that they are against your idea because they love you. They regard their hostile remarks as being for your own good. You are going to have to manoeuvre your way through the minefield of family hostility, and find alternative sources of emotional support. You need to truthfully ask yourself whether you can withstand their attitude.

4   You asked yourself whether you understand the difference between the world of employment and the world of self-employment.

These are two different planets. The inhabitants of these planets speak different languages. They have different habits. They have different ways of looking at themselves, at the world, and at the concept of work. Are you sure you're able to make the switch? Can you submit yourself to deprogramming, and can you take on board a whole new mindset?

5   You asked yourself whether you are prepared for the loneliness that accompanies any new start-up.

Loneliness is axiomatic. It is an integral part of the entrepreneurial experience. Are you emotionally ready for the sense of isolation that inevitably accompanies you as you strike out on your own? Are you going to be able to overcome the loneliness and find the motivation to get out there, day after day, and promote your business? Once the excitement and adrenalin of establishing your new venture wears off, you are on your own. You must honestly assess whether you're ready for this.

6   You asked yourself whether you are the right age to start your own business.

This is a no-brainer. Of course you are the right age. I read somewhere that for knowledge intensive sectors, the average age of entrepreneurs is 37.6 years. I wonder if this means that someone aged 37.7 years is over the hill? Or if someone aged 37.5 should wait a few more weeks? Naturally, as you grow older, you simply trade one set of advantages for another. Young people are likely to have more energy, more free time and less family ties, while older people might have had more time to accumulate funds and assets for their new business. But essentially, the age issue is meaningless babble. There is no best age to start a business.

7   You asked yourself what field of business you should choose.

In this book, we have made a critical distinction between entrepreneurial skills and the entrepreneurial mindset. I believe strongly that the mindset must come before the skills. But once you decide to start your own business, you have to decide what business. This is crunch time. In what field will you make your mark? This is the stage where you must develop and finalise your business idea.

8   You asked yourself whether you should work from home.

Even if you choose a type of business that can be run from home, you still need to check whether emotionally this makes sense for you. Can you muster the necessary self-discipline? Can you set boundaries for yourself and for anyone else in the family home – including the dog? Can you convince your fellow house-mates that you need physical and emotional space if you are to successfully run your business from your home?

9   You asked yourself whether you have the right mix of entrepreneurial qualities to be your own boss.

The fact that so many different experts suggest so many different combinations of 'must-have' entrepreneurial qualities should cause you no anxiety. Everyone instinctively knows what these qualities are. You don't need a perfect score on every entrepreneurial quality ever suggested! What you do need is a sensible mix of qualities. You will often find that a surplus of one quality makes up for the absence of other qualities. For example, supreme confidence in your ability to overcome adversity, and boundless energy to bulldoze your way past obstacles, may often be sufficient to get you to where you want to go.

10 You asked yourself whether you have enough passion, fire in the belly and chutzpah.

If you are not passionate about your business, don't bother. If you don't have fire in the belly, you may run out of entrepreneurial steam. You will need plenty of passion and plenty of fire in the belly if you want to survive the roller-coaster entrepreneurial experience. Your business is your baby. Nurture it. Protect it. And if you want your business to really stand out from the competition, add chutzpah to the mix. Push the boundaries. Catch the competition off guard.

Having asked yourself these 10 questions, you are in a better emotional state to make a decision about whether to start your own business or not.

The fact that I always encourage people with the right balance of fire in the belly and business aptitude to go it alone, does not mean that there is anything wrong with remaining in the corporate world. Only you can decide where your comfort zone lies.

The huge choice of business resources – books, websites, enterprise support agencies – available to aspiring entrepreneurs, has not significantly reduced the business failure rate. This is because the ability to produce a sparkling business plan is less important than the ability to handle the anxiety associated with going out on your own.

If you decide that you definitely want to leave your ladder job and start your own business, here's a word of advice: don't burn your bridges. We all remember the scene from the movie Jerry Maguire, where the hero has been unceremoniously fired. He delivers a profanity-laden tirade against his boss and his co-workers. Don't be tempted!

- *Don't antagonise your former boss.*
- *Don't badmouth your former colleagues.*
- *Don't make unauthorised phone calls on company time.*
- *Don't send your CV through the company's email.*

You never know when you might need your employer again, or when your employer may need you again. It's worth developing a smooth exit strategy that leaves the door open for continued dialogue and future co-operation.

Don't alienate the movers and shakers in your industry. Always try and discuss a "What if . . . ?" scenario with your boss. Be smart, and learn what information and contacts you can and cannot take with you. In particular, seek ways of turning your former employer into your first client.

CASE STUDY

The first job that William Teel got after he left college was writing software at the US Department of Energy. Six years later, he left the department to start his own company, 1 Source Consulting. He got his first contract for $10,000 *from the DOE. In the years that followed, William's decision to maintain close links with his former employer resulted in him being awarded more business from the DOE, including his first major contract for $3 million.*

In 2003, 1 Source Solutions beat off some of the largest corporations in America to win a contract to take over the DOE's entire IT infrastructure. The seven-year contract was worth more than $1 billion, and was one of the largest government contracts ever awarded to a small company.

It is also worth remembering that very few entrepreneurs know exactly what they're doing from day 1. Look at successful companies like Ford, GE, Dyson, Google, Yahoo!, Microsoft, Flickr, Hershey, Dell, and Sun. Their founders had dreams. They had plans. They had ambition.

But when they first started out, they had no way of knowing for certain which direction their company would go, or whether they would be so successful.

The 10 key questions that we posed in this book are designed to help you decide whether you can make the emotional switch from employee status to self-employed status. You need to be sure that you have the emotional endurance and the emotional stamina to see your journey through.

If you are happy with your answers to these questions, if you are convinced that the entrepreneurial life is for you, then I believe you are ready to successfully navigate the transition from ladder mindset to entrepreneurial mindset.

As you prepare to embrace this transition, give some thought to covering any business skill deficiencies. Attend training courses, seek advice from experts, and hire people with the necessary skills. It is also useful to immerse yourself in entrepreneurial pursuits like reading business books and magazines, visiting entrepreneurial websites, and being inspired by the stories of other entrepreneurs.

As you embark on your own entrepreneurial odyssey, all that remains for me is to wish you:

Bon Voyage!

Also by TheExcellenceForum

Graduate to Success
By
James Sweetman

Graduate to Success is a guidebook for those who want to soar in their careers. James Sweetman, a leading Business, Personal & Performance Coach inspires, supports and challenges you to unlock the door to your potential. The book shows you how to -
- ✓ Connect with your passions in life
- ✓ Design an action plan for your career success
- ✓ Create your own personal brand
- ✓ Learn strategies to sprint up the career ladder

"Read this book to be reassured, to be inspired and to find the way to your own heart and then, how to follow it." Nick Williams, best-selling author of 'The Work You Were Born To Do.'

www.theexcellenceforum.com